TONGUES OF
FIRE

Destiny Image Books by Jennifer LeClaire

Cleansing Your Home from Evil

The Making of a Watchman

Decoding the Mysteries of Heaven's War Room

Discerning Prophetic Witchcraft

Your End Times Prayer Secret

Victory Decrees

The Seer Dimensions

The Spiritual Warrior's Guide to Defeating Water Spirits

The Prophet's Devotional

TONGUES OF FIRE

101 SUPERNATURAL BENEFITS OF PRAYING IN THE HOLY SPIRIT

JENNIFER LECLAIRE

DESTINY IMAGE® PUBLISHERS, INC.
P.O. Box 310, Shippensburg, PA 17257-0310
"Promoting Inspired Lives."

This book and all other Destiny Image and Destiny Image Fiction books are available at Christian bookstores and distributors worldwide.

Cover design by Eileen Rockwell.

For more information on foreign distributors, call 717-532-3040.

Reach us on the Internet: www.destinyimage.com.

ISBN 13 TP: 978-0-7684-6211-1

ISBN 13 eBook: 978-0-7684-6212-8

ISBN 13 HC: 978-0-7684-6214-2

ISBN 13 LP: 978-0-7684-6213-5

For Worldwide Distribution, Printed in the U.S.A.

2 3 4 5 6 7 8 / 26 25 24 23 22

ACKNOWLEDGMENTS

I am grateful to my Awakening House of Prayer Global Movement family of prayer houses, house churches, churches, and prayer hubs. Thanks for your fervent prayers over this book. I'm grateful for the publishing team at Destiny Image, including publisher Larry Sparks, who suggested my teachings on this topic should be in book form, as well as Tina Pugh, Shaun Tabatt, and Eileen Rockwell who designed an awesome cover.

DEDICATION

I dedicate this book to my friend, praying John. John Angelini prayed more than us all. He was a faithful intercessor for the ministry who went home to be with the Lord and left a legacy of love, kindness, patience, and generosity. Thank you, John, for praying without ceasing and for helping to make it possible to travel the world preaching the gospel, raising up intercessors, and equipping prophets. I couldn't have done it without you, and you will be sorely missed. I'll see you on the other side.

CONTENTS

101 Supernatural Benefits of Praying in the Holy Spirit

BY BILL HAMON

God's greatest gift to the world was His own Son for the redemption of mankind. Jesus gave the Holy Spirit to the church as His greatest gift after He ascended back to heaven. The Holy Spirit gave the greatest gift He could give to the individual saints, their own spirit language called unknown tongues and other tongues. It is a gift to the inner-born-again spirit person called the inner man. Thank God Jennifer LeClaire has done a beautiful job of showing the importance and great value this gift is to the believer. She presents it in a little different format than I do in my book, *70 Reasons for Speaking in Tongues.* In 2012, I wrote the book on the Third Reformation and Great Awakening. Then the Lord told me to write the book that would help the church to fulfill God's purpose for the Third Reformation and activate the Great Awakening. In that book, I give 70 benefits and purposes for praying with our spirit language

In my 68 years of ministry in the Holy Spirit, I discovered that Christians who have received the gift of their own spirit language use it less than 10% to appropriate all the benefits, power, and blessings produced by praying in tongues. When the Holy Spirit deposits the gift of the spirit language into a Christian, it is like someone depositing a million dollars into your bank account, but you only write five- and ten-dollar checks occasionally.

Jennifer reveals over 101 benefits your gift can produce for you. There are unlimited benefits to praying in tongues. There are also judgments from God for not using your gift of tongues. Paul admonished Timothy to stir up that gift which is in him (see 2 Tim. 1:6). The master pronounced judgment on one of his servants who never used the gift that was given to him (see Matt. 25:24-29) and Hebrews 2:3 says "how shall we escape" if we neglect to use the gift God has given.

I encourage you to read this book and practice the truths about using your spirit language. Jesus died to redeem us from our sins by shedding His life's blood when He died on the cross. Jesus declared to His apostles that it would be more profitable for them if He died and went to be with His Father, for then He could send them the promise of the Father—the Holy Spirit gift of their own spirit language could be given to each child of God.

Every Christian needs to read and study this book to be a victorious Christian by having the gift that enables them to activate any of the gifts and graces of Jesus Christ.

—**Bishop Bill Hamon**
Bishop: Christian International Apostolic-Global Network
Author: *The Eternal Church, Prophets & Personal Prophecy, Prophets & the Prophetic Movement, Prophets, Pitfalls, & Principles, Apostles/Prophets & the Coming Moves of God, The Day of the Saints, Who Am I & Why Am I Here, The Final Reformation & Great Awaking, 70 Reasons for Speaking in Tongues, and How Can These Things Be? God's Weapons of War, Your Highest Calling*

CHAPTER 1

A 90-DAY PRAYER
CHALLENGE

It came out of nowhere. It was certainly unexpected, but it was a clear mandate from the Lord. It happened on my *Mornings with the Holy Spirit* daily prayer broadcast—an hour of prophetic intercession, prophecy, and decrees. I felt the Holy Spirit stirring me, and suddenly a spontaneous prophecy erupted that charged the Body of Christ to pray in tongues for an hour a day for 90 days. I heard the Lord say:

> Pray in My Spirit and I will do a work on the inside of you that will birth miracles in you and miracles through you. Pray in the Spirit. That is the master key that so many of My children are missing. For they read the Word, read the Word, read the Word, read the Word, which does so much good in their soul, but when they begin to pray in the Spirit in conjunction with reading the Word, a revival begins to break out in their heart that spills over into their words, into their cities and churches, and the lost begin to take notice.
>
> I'm supercharging you even now as you pray in the Spirit. So do not delay by putting off this vital aspect of your life in Christ any longer. But begin to walk like He walked as you talk like He talked and think like He thinks and pray like

He prayed, going off to secret places early in the morning, waiting on Me for direction, only doing what He saw Me do.

Do it my way. I won't do it your way, but I'll help you do it My way. I have a life of power, of prophetic wonder for you. So stand firm in My promises and do not budge from the place that I've called you to stand, and pray in the Spirit and speak the Word only and watch what happens when you combine this with that, the Word with the Spirit. Watch the revival that breaks out in your heart and in your mind, in your soul, in your emotions, every bit of you. You will begin to burn and shine for Me and the world will stand up and take notice.

Over the next 90 days, if you will commit yourself to praying in the Sprit full on, I will do miracles on the inside of you and I will even change circumstances on the outside. If you'll just pray in the Spirit, you'll see that some of those circumstances on the outside won't bother you on the inside and some of those things on the inside will have to come out and go to the outside because they don't belong in you. And if you'll let Me mortify that inner life, the part that is warring against My Spirit, those places that are infiltrated by the enemy's lies, you will see new life will spring forth. Ninety days to a better you.

Proven Breakthrough Prayer Power

From that powerful prophetic word, I started teaching day by day on praying in tongues. That teaching extended beyond 90 days, and we saw testimonies roll in from all over the world of breakthroughs in just about every area one could want a breakthrough.

Darlene wrote, "I've noticed that since I've been praying in tongues, fear is vanishing. I'm strengthened in mind, body, and soul!" Margaret wrote in about a stunning manifestation: "I have noticed an increase in divine appointments (seeing people I know, prayer burdens, divine intervention), and I have also received an increase in prophetic messages from God."

Veronique told us, "My hope has increased. I know that the Lord is doing a great work in me even if I do not quite know what it is right now." Angela related, "Discernment has kicked in even more. I have seen miracles and look forward to seeing more!" And Kim said, "In just the short time, my heart is changing, mindset has changed, stable thinking abilities, and relationship with my husband getting better."

Multitask Prayer Revealed

When we pray in tongues, many things may be happening at the same time. God can be giving us more wisdom and strengthening us simultaneously. We could be building up our faith and growing in the gifts of the Spirit—or the fruit of the Spirit—at the same time. I believe when we pray in tongues with our mind set on a specific purpose, the Holy Spirit helps us release the perfect prayer to bring that God-ordained purpose to pass.

The more I studied what happens—or what can happen—when we pray in tongues, the more inspiration I found to continue the charge and press into the benefits. The fruit of praying in tongues is sometimes immediate. Praying in tongues sometimes serves as what I like to call preventative maintenance. In other words, if you pray in tongues with a mind to cultivate boldness, the boldness will be there when you need it.

Put another way, praying in tongues is sometimes, but not always, about what you need in the moment. The Holy Spirit knows what you need before you need it, and because praying in tongues releases the perfect prayer (see Rom. 8:26-27) we may be pleasantly surprised with the results even if they don't manifest in the moment. Praying in tongues brings personal transformation, builds our capacity for God, and so, so much more.

At the same time, we may not put two and two together. We may not always discern that it was our tongues prayer that brought the breakthrough. Because we can't always understand our tongues prayer, we often have no idea what we're praying. In fact, I believe we pray prayers in tongues that we wouldn't dare pray in English, such as, "Lord, crucify my flesh!"

Here's what I know, if praying in tongues an hour a day for 90 days brought breakthrough to so many people around the world—and it did—what would happen if we adopted a lifestyle of tongues prayer? What if we developed the habit—the discipline—of praying in tongues daily? I believe the primary reason we don't pray in tongues more is because we lack a revelation of what really happens—and what is possible—when we consistently release our tongues prayer. This book will give you that revelation and build your faith to pray in tongues. The results will indeed be miraculous.

CHAPTER 2

FILLED WITH
THE SPIRIT

ave you ever been filled with the Holy Spirit? When you were
saved, the Holy Spirit came to live on the inside of you. But
there's a difference between receiving the Holy Spirit at conver-
sion and being filled with the Spirit. Jesus spoke of the latter experience
in John 14:16-17:

> *And I will pray the Father, and He will give you another*
> *Helper, that He may abide with you forever—the Spirit of*
> *truth, whom the world cannot receive, because it neither sees*
> *Him nor knows Him; but you know Him, for He dwells with*
> *you and will be in you.*

Even if you have been filled with the Holy Spirit in the past, we see
biblically that this glorious infilling is not a one-time event. Christians
can be a little leaky at times. Maybe you need to get refilled. We see the
apostles in Scripture filled three different times. And Paul the apostle
wrote, "And do not be drunk with wine, in which is dissipation; but be
filled with the Spirit, speaking to one another in psalms and hymns and
spiritual songs, singing and making melody in your heart to the Lord"
(Eph. 5:18-19).

The Holy Spirit Is a Gift from the Father

The first step to getting filled with the Spirit of God is to see that He is a gift from the Father, first given on the Day of Pentecost. This wasn't intended to be a one-time-only event for that generation. The gift of the Holy Spirit has been available to all Christians since that time, and He is available to you now. Let's look at the original outpouring in Acts 2:1-4:

> When the Day of Pentecost had fully come, they were all with one accord in one place. And suddenly there came a sound from heaven, as of a rushing mighty wind, and it filled the whole house where they were sitting. Then there appeared to them divided tongues, as of fire, and one sat upon each of them. And they were all filled with the Holy Spirit and began to speak with other tongues, as the Spirit gave them utterance.

You receive the baptism of the Holy Spirit by faith, just like you received your salvation. We don't have to beg God to give us the Holy Spirit. We don't have to "tarry" (wait) for days and years. Faith doesn't beg. Faith believes and receives. Peter offered these words in Acts 2:38: "Repent, and let every one of you be baptized in the name of Jesus Christ for the remission of sins; and you shall receive the gift of the Holy Spirit."

Your Perfection Is Not a Prerequisite

You don't have to be living perfectly to receive the Holy Spirit any more than you needed to be living perfectly to get saved. The Holy Spirit Himself perfects you little by little. He sanctifies you little by little. He is your Helper and wants to help you. He can help you more if you are filled with Him. Jesus said in Luke 11:11-13:

If a son asks for bread from any father among you, will he give him a stone? Or if he asks for a fish, will he give him a serpent instead of a fish? Or if he asks for an egg, will he offer him a scorpion? If you then, being evil, know how to give good gifts to your children, how much more will your heavenly Father give the Holy Spirit to those who ask Him!

You become a son when you accept Jesus. As sons, we don't work for the Holy Spirit. We receive Him as a gift from the Father, as another Comforter that Christ talked about.

Methods of Receiving the Baptism

You can receive the Holy Spirit through the laying on of hands, but that's not the only way. Back in the Voice of Healing days, Oral Roberts and other evangelists who broadcasted their meetings over the airwaves would tell people to put their hands on the TV screen as a point of contact.

I was baptized in the Holy Spirit at a Joyce Meyer conference. No one laid hands on me at all. We see this type of baptism in the Holy Spirit in Acts 10:44-46:

While Peter was still speaking these words, the Holy Spirit fell upon all those who heard the word. And those of the circumcision who believed were astonished, as many as came with Peter, because the gift of the Holy Spirit had been poured out on the Gentiles also. For they heard them speak with tongues and magnify God.

Receive by Faith

When you ask for the baptism of the Holy Spirit, you will have to yield to Him.

You will have to take a step of faith. When you ask Jesus to baptize you in the Holy Spirit, you may feel a bubbling up in your spirit. Or you may feel tingly or warmth. Or maybe you won't feel anything. I didn't.

After you pray, you'll have to open your mouth and yield it to the Holy Spirit. You do the talking as the Holy Spirit gives you utterance. Psalm 81:10 says, "Open your mouth wide, and I will fill it." Open your mouth and release your voice to the Holy Spirit. It may sound at first like baby talk or gibberish. That's OK.

Just like a baby's language grows and develops, so will your prayer language grow and develop over time. Remember, we are speaking. The Holy Spirit is not speaking. We are speaking and He is giving us utterance. An utterance is "a vocal expression, power, style, or manner of speaking," according to *Merriam-Webster*'s dictionary.

A Prayer for the Baptism of the Holy Spirit

If you want to be filled with the Holy Spirit, pray this prayer:

> Father, I surrender full control of my life to You. I ask You even now to fill me to overflowing with Your Spirit, just as You have promised to do if I ask according to Your will. I ask this in the name of Jesus and believe that You are pouring out Your Spirit upon me right now.

Now take a deep breath as if you are breathing in the Holy Spirit. I often tell people to drink deep. Jesus told people to come and drink, and

He was speaking of drinking of the river of life, which you breathe in. Again, open your mouth and He will fill it.

If nothing seems to be happening, relax and don't get in your mind about it. Don't get into unbelief about it. Sometimes you'll hear the words on the inside and you have to give voice to them. Speak out in faith—and keep speaking. You can then pray in tongues any time you choose.

CHAPTER 3

YOUR HEAVENLY
PRAYER
LANGUAGE

When I was in high school I took three years of Latin against the advice of my parents, who wanted me to learn Spanish. After all, you can't really speak Latin in the modern world. Well, I suppose I could have, but nobody in the modern world would have understood me. I may as well have been speaking in tongues. Now, I do.

Paul the apostle shared a marvelous revelation in First Corinthians 14:2 (MEV), "For he who speaks in an *unknown* tongue does not speak to men, but to God. For no one understands him, although in the spirit, he speaks mysteries." The word *unknown* in this verse is in italics because it doesn't appear in the original text. Translators added in the word "unknown" for clarity.

That's partly accurate. When we speak in tongues, we are speaking in a language that is not known to mankind. That's quite something, given that there are over 7,000 known languages in the world today, according to Ethnologue. (That's why Bible translators are so busy!) So, yes, in that sense it's an unknown tongue on earth. But it's not an unknown tongue in heaven. In fact, it's a heavenly language.

If I were to call you on the phone, I would not speak to you in tongues because you could not understand me. When I teach at my Ft. Lauderdale church, Awakening House of Prayer, I do not teach in tongues because that would not build you up. Paul said, "Yet in the church I would rather speak five words with my understanding, that I may teach others also, than ten thousand words in a tongue" (1 Cor. 14:19).

When you speak in your heavenly language, God understands you perfectly. It's probable no one else on the face of the earth understands a word you are saying. And you may have noticed your tongues for personal edification sound different than other people's tongues for personal edification. God gave you a unique prayer language just like you have a unique fingerprint.

Have you ever been concerned about people eavesdropping on you while you are praying? When you pray in tongues, you don't have to be concerned because nobody can understand you.

I pray in the Spirit as much as I possibly can. I wake up most mornings and pray at least 30 minutes in the Spirit before doing anything else. (I used to pray in the Spirit while I was trying to go to sleep but it kept me up because it energized me!) I accomplish this by praying in the Spirit from the moment my feet hit the ground, while I'm in the shower, while I'm making my coffee, etc. The time flies!

I pray in the Spirit while I am in my car. I even broke out in tongues on the treadmill at the gym accidentally—because it's automatic—and everyone started to stare at me! I have sticky notes in certain parts of my house that say "Pray in tongues" to remind myself lest I forget. When the handyman or other workers come to fix things, they aren't sure what to think about those sticky notes. But I don't care.

I'm not telling you this to create a law, but to encourage you to allow praying in the Spirit to become so natural that your immediate response in times of need is to lift up Spirit-led prayers. When something bad happens—or sometimes when something good happens—I immediately burst out in tongues. When you yield your tongue to the Holy Spirit, you will too.

Prayer

Father, in the name of Jesus, would You remind me to pray in the Spirit? Help me to make praying in the Spirit a Holy Ghost habit that becomes automatic when I wake up in the morning and as I walk through my day. I yield my tongue to the heavenly language You have given me.

CHAPTER 4

EFFECTIVE, FERVENT TONGUES

James, the apostle of practical faith, shares some wisdom in the fifth chapter of the book that goes by his name. James 5:16 tells us, "The effective, fervent prayer of a righteous man avails much." If you can pray effectively, that means you can pray ineffectively. Likewise, if you can pray in the spirit effectively, you can pray in the spirit ineffectively.

I like the Amplified Bible translation of this verse: "The heartfelt and persistent prayer of a righteous man (believer) can accomplish much [when put into action and made effective by God—it is dynamic and can have tremendous power]."

The Amplified version gives you more insight into what *effectively* means—heartfelt and persistent. Other translations use the word *earnest, urgent, continual,* and *insistent*. You can feel the passion in those words, and it's with passion we should pray in the spirit.

Many people have told me, "I pray in tongues in my head." Let me correct this belief. You can't pray in tongues inside your head. You may hear tongues inside your head, but you have to give voice to the Holy Spirit's utterance. You don't have to pray loud. You are talking directly to God. He can hear you. You can speak softly. You can even whisper.

Tongues make noise. That's why it's often called speaking in tongues. You can pray other ways in your head because God hears everything, but you must pray in tongues audibly, even if it's just a quiet whisper, as you are yielding your tongue to the Spirit of God who is praying with you.

God Himself sometimes speaks to us in a still small voice (see 1 Kings 19:11-13). Likewise, God whispers to us in our dreams (see Job 33:15). You are not effectively praying in tongues if you are not expressing the prayer verbally. Again, you can't pray in tongues in your head. You have to put your natural tongue in motion.

You can pray loud if you want to. Sometimes passion will cause you to pray loud. Many times when I pray in the spirit I am loud and demonstrative. Sometimes the Holy Spirit is more fervent about a thing and you will feel that fervency and get louder or even demonstrative. Let the Holy Spirit lead you.

Prayer

Father, in the name of Jesus, help me to flow with You in my spirit prayer life. Show me the prayer power I am releasing when I yield my tongue to Your utterance in prayer so I can pray effectively, fervently, earnestly, urgently, continually, and insistently.

CHAPTER 5

YOUR BRAIN
ON TONGUES

Remember the "Your Brain on Drugs" campaign? The 1980s initiative by Partnership for a Drug-Free America aimed to help people understand what happens when people take drugs. The commercials show a man holding up an egg saying, "This is your brain." He then points to a frying pan and says, "This is drugs." Next, he cracks open the egg over a frying pain and, as the eggs start sizzling, he says, "This is your brain on drugs."

Dr. Andrew Newberg, a University of Pennsylvania researcher, released study findings that prove the reality of Holy Spirit-inspired tongues. He did this by monitoring the brain activity of people as they prayed in tongues. Newberg concluded our heavenly language is not a natural language because the frontal lobe of the brain—where natural languages originates—is not activated in brain scans when people are praying in tongues.

Dr. Caroline Leaf, a neuroscientist and born-again believer, indicates speaking in tongues increases mental health and emotional stability. She said, "When we speak in tongues, the frontal lobe of the brain, which is involved in intentionality, decreases in activity showing that we are not consciously controlling the process."

Newberg told ABC News, "When they are actually engaged in this whole very intense spiritual practice for them, their frontal lobes tend to go down in activity, but I think it's very consistent with the kind of experience that they have because they say that they are not in charge—it's the voice of God, the Spirit of God that's moving through them."[1]

Newberg's study co-author, Donna Morgan, a born-again Christian who says she considers the ability to speak in tongues a gift, told *The New York Times*, "You're aware of your surroundings. You're not really out of control. But you have no control over what's happening. You're just flowing. You're in a realm of peace and comfort, and it's a fantastic feeling."[2]

So, if you needed science to back up your faith you have it. You don't have to get into your head about praying in tongues. But know that it does impact your brain in a positive way, literally renewing your mind.

Prayer

Father, in the name of Jesus, help me not get into my head about praying in tongues. Help me rest in faith knowing that You are really speaking and praying through me so I will be encouraged to lean into my heavenly language all the more.

Notes

1. "Speaking in Tongues Medical Study proves Holy Spirit praying," YouTube, Jul 18, 2008, https://www.youtube.com/watch?v=NZbQBajYnEc1.

2. Benedict Carey, "A Neuroscientific Look at Speaking in Tongues," November 7, 2006, https://www.nytimes.com/2006/11/07/health/07brain.html.

101 SUPERNATURAL
BENEFITS
OF PRAYING IN THE HOLY SPIRIT

BENEFIT 1

Build Yourself Up

I am always amazed at how God sets us up for success. When we got born again, God gave us the measure of faith to walk in our calling (see Rom. 12:3). We all received the same measure of faith, so we all started out on equal footing.

But God doesn't stop there. He helps us to grow in our faith by giving us His Word so we can build faith in His great and precious promises (see 2 Pet. 1:4). Paul told us faith comes by hearing and hearing by the Word of God (see Rom. 10:17).

But hearing God's Word is not the only way we build our measure of faith. And that's important because we cannot spend all day in the Word. We have to work, shop, do laundry, and so on. God knows that. So in His wisdom He gave us yet another means to extend our measure. You can pray in tongues in church, while you are reading the Word, while you are cooking dinner, and many other times of the day.

We can build our faith through praying in tongues. Jude 20 (MEV) says, "But you, beloved, build yourselves up in your most holy faith. Pray in the Holy Spirit." The Amplified Classic version of this Scripture puts it this way: "But you, beloved, build yourselves up [founded] on your most holy faith [make progress, rise like an edifice higher and higher], praying in the Holy Spirit."

To build up is "to develop gradually by increments, to promote the health, strength, esteem, or reputation of, to accumulate or develop appreciably," according to *Merriam-Webster*'s dictionary. When I was in Malaysia, I went to the top of the tallest building in the world. My ears actually popped on the way to the top. I want my faith to ascend so high my spiritual ears pop!

Let's look at *The Passion Translation* of this verse: "But you, my delightfully loved friends, constantly and progressively build yourselves up on the foundation of your most holy faith by praying every moment in the Spirit." And *The Message*, "But you, dear friends, carefully build yourselves up in this most holy faith by praying in the Holy Spirit, staying right at the center of God's love, keeping your arms open and outstretched, ready for the mercy of our Master, Jesus Christ."

Your most holy faith is pure faith. It's not diluted with fear and doubt and unbelief. When you pray in tongues you root out the fear, doubt, and unbelief. You are purifying your heart. You are building your faith. When you pray in tongues you are perfecting your faith. This happens little by little, in the same way you build muscles little by little in the gym.

Prayer

Father, in the name of Jesus, help me put my trust on the reality that when I pray in tongues I am literally building my faith. Help me to have faith in the process of my spiritual development as I release my tongues for edification.

BENEFIT 2

Tongues, Miracles, Signs, and Wonders

B ishop Bill Hamon, my spiritual father, says the gift of the Holy Spirit is the mother of all miracles. That's something to ponder as we understand our tongue is the most powerful member in the human body. The tongue can sanctify the body for God's use or set it on hell's fire for the devil's use. James told us, "But no man can tame the tongue. It is an unruly evil, full of deadly poison" (James 3:8).

"No man can tame the tongue, but God can. When God baptizes a person in the Holy Spirit, He tames the tongue by having it speak the language of His Spirit," Hamon wrote in his book, *70 Reasons for Speaking in Tongues*. "It takes great faith and trust in God to allow Him to have us speak in a heavenly spirit language that our mind does not understand or know what is being spoken."[1]

Kenneth E. Hagin, the late father of the Word of Faith movement, called tongues "a vocal miracle."[2] Dick Iverson, founding pastor of City Bible Church said, "It is a direct manifestation of the miraculous."[3] Just think about it. When you speak in tongues it is God Himself speaking and praying through you in a language nobody understands but you and Him (and anyone He may allow to translate the tongue).

Sunday Adelaja, founder and senior pastor of the Embassy of the Blessed Kingdom of God for All Nations, an evangelical-charismatic megachurch, once said this: "Tongues are a miraculous manifestation of being filled with the Holy Ghost."

Not only is praying in tongues a miracle in itself, I believe—and can speak through experience—that praying in tongues leads to the manifestation of miracles, signs, and wonders in us and through us. Think about it. The power of death and life are in your tongue (see Prov. 18:21).

Many times we speak death over our lives and hinder God's miracle-working power. When the angel Gabriel told Zechariah that Elizabeth was pregnant, he spoke out in unbelief. To prevent the priest from cursing God's promise, Gabriel muted him for nine months. He was only able to speak after John the Baptist was born.

God is not going to mute our mouths, but catch this: Many times we get frustrated waiting for the miracles and the enemy puts pressure on our tongues. By praying in tongues, we can avoid saying something that hinders God's miracle-working power in our life. We are giving God the reins of our heart and God is sanctifying our tongue.

Beyond your own miracles, I believe praying in tongues positions us to tap into God's wonder-working power. Jesus said signs would follow those who believe. Praying in tongues helps us get the unbelief out of our minds, out of our hearts, and out of our mouth so we can release the Kingdom of God with authority.

Prayer

Father, in the name of Jesus, help me tap into the miracle-working power of Your Spirit by yielding my tongue to Your utterance. Prepare me from the inside out to believe for miracles, receive miracles, and release miracles in the earth for Your glory.

Notes

1. Bill Hamon, *70 Reasons for Speaking in Tongues* (Shippensburg, PA: Destiny Image Publishers, 2012).

2. Kenneth Hagin, *The Holy Spirit and His Gifts* (Tulsa, OK: Kenneth Hagin Ministries, 1991), 149.

3. Dick Iverson, *The Holy Spirit Today* (Portland, OR: City Bible Publishing, 2006), 175.

When You Don't Know How to Pray

Paul offers a revelation that can change your entire life in Romans 8:26: "Likewise, the Spirit helps us in our weaknesses, for we do not know what to pray for as we ought, but the Spirit Himself intercedes for us with groanings too deep for words" (MEV).

We may think we know how to pray, and sometimes we do, but many times we don't have a clue what prayer answer we really need. If the Holy Spirit tells us how to pray, we can pray effectively in our natural language. If we have a promise from God in the Word, we can apply it through prayer to a situation.

However, if you are not getting prayer answers, consider what James 4:3 says about "asking amiss." The Greek word for *amiss* in the context of this Scripture means "improperly" or "wrongly." If you are praying wrongly, you won't get the right answers—or perhaps any answer.

I like *The Passion Translation* of Romans 8:26: "And in a similar way, the Holy Spirit takes hold of us in our human frailty to empower us in our weakness. For example, at times we don't even know how to pray, or know the best things to ask for. But the Holy Spirit rises up within us to super-intercede on our behalf, pleading to God with emotional sighs too deep for words."

The Message translation puts it this way: "If we don't know how or what to pray, it doesn't matter. He does our praying in and for us, making prayer out of our wordless sighs, our aching groans. He knows us far better than we know ourselves, knows our pregnant condition, and keeps us present before God. That's why we can be so sure that every detail in our lives of love for God is worked into something good."

And the Amplified Classic: "So too the [Holy] Spirit comes to our aid and bears us up in our weakness; for we do not know what prayer to offer nor how to offer it worthily as we ought, but the Spirit Himself goes to meet our supplication and pleads in our behalf with unspeakable yearnings and groanings too deep for utterance."

Why am I repeating this Scripture over and over? Because I want it to sink in. Again, we may think we know how to pray, and sometimes we do, but many times we don't have a clue what prayer answer we really need. Notice also that Romans 8:26 is in the context of Romans 8:27-28, which tells us, "Now He who searches the hearts knows what the mind of the Spirit is, because He makes intercession for the saints according to the will of God. And we know that all things work together for good to those who love God, to those who are the called according to His purpose."

If you want something bad to work out for your good, pray. And when you don't know how to pray—which is more often than we think—pray in tongues. The Holy Spirit knows how to take what the enemy meant for harm and turn it for your good (see Gen. 50:20).

Prayer

Father, in the name of Jesus, help me remember to lean on You, acknowledging You in my prayer closet. When I am frustrated, help me get out of my head and into Your heart, giving voice to Your utterance so You can help me see Your will come to pass in my life.

Tapping into Heaven's Revelation

P aul said he was glad he spoke in tongues more than anyone (see 1 Cor. 14:18). The Amplified Classic version reads, "I thank God that I speak in [strange] tongues (languages) more than any of you *or* all of you put together."

Have you ever wondered why? Have you ever considered the fruit of Paul's spirit-prayer life? There was abounding fruit, to be sure, and part of that fruit was revelation.

Let's look at some definitions of *revelation*. *Merriam-Webster's* defines *revelation* as an act of revealing or communicating divine truth, something that is revealed by God to human, an act of revealing to view or making known.

The King James New Testament Greek Lexicon defines *revelation* as "disclosure of truth, instruction; concerning things before unknown, used of events by which things or states or persons hitherto withdrawn from view are made visible to all."

Paul wrote two thirds of the New Testament by direct revelation from heaven. I believe praying in tongues unlocked some of that revelation. Paul spoke of how Jesus made known to him mysteries through revelation (see Eph. 3:3). Flesh and blood did not reveal the mysteries Paul wrote about in Scripture. It was the Spirit of God, and I believe Paul tapped into that heavenly revelation, in part, through his habit of praying in tongues.

Paul explained, "It is doubtless not profitable for me to boast. I will come to visions and revelations of the Lord: I know a man in Christ who fourteen years ago—whether in the body I do not know, or whether out of the body I do not know, God knows—such a one was caught up to the third heaven" (2 Cor. 12:1-2).

Paul walked in so much revelation, God had to make sure pride didn't enter into his heart. Can you imagine walking in that much revelation? Paul explained, "And lest I should be exalted above measure by the abundance of the revelations, a thorn in the flesh was given to me, a messenger of Satan to buffet me, lest I be exalted above measure" (2 Cor. 12:7).

Paul moved by revelation time and time again. In Galatians 2:2 he shared, "And I went up by revelation, and communicated to them that gospel which I preach among the Gentiles, but privately to those who were of reputation, lest by any means I might run, or had run, in vain." He told the Corinthians he would "come to visions and revelations of the Lord."

When God gave me the revelation of praying in tongues for the sake of revelation, I prayed in tongues non-stop for a year. The fruit of that book was a revelation from the Book of Mark that became a book called *Developing Faith for the Working of Miracles*.

Heaven's revelation may come to you in many forms. It can come as the word of the Lord speaking to your heart, through dreams, impressions, visions, trances, out-of-body experiences. We know Paul moved in all those seer dimensions. Praying in tongues doesn't promise these encounters, but it does prime the pump for prophetic revelation and inspiration.

Pray in tongues. Don't neglect the Word of God. The Spirit and the Word agree. Choose to live, move, and have your being in the Revelator who leads you and guides you.

Prayer

Father, in the name of Jesus, would You give me the spirit of wisdom and revelation in the knowledge of Christ? Will You promote me to pray in tongues to unlocks heaven's revelation for my life? I want to walk in abundant revelation.

Praying the Perfect Prayer

We know that we know that we know that sometimes we don't know how to pray as we ought. But we also know the secret to praying the perfect prayer. That secret is outlined in Romans 8:27, "He who searches the hearts knows what the mind of the Spirit is, because He intercedes for the saints according to the will of God" (MEV).

The Amplified Classic version reads, "And He Who searches the hearts of men knows what is in the mind of the [Holy] Spirit [what His intent is], because the Spirit intercedes and pleads [before God] in behalf of the saints according to and in harmony with God's will."

God the Holy Spirit always knows what God the Father thinks. God the Holy Spirit always knows what God the Father wants. When you pray in tongues, the Holy Spirit is actually pleading your case or need to the Father in such a way that the Father hears and answers.

The Contemporary English Version tells us, "All of our thoughts are known to God. He can understand what is in the mind of the Spirit, as the Spirit prays for God's people." The Holy Spirit has the mind of God. He always knows the perfect will of the Father and always gets His prayers answered. Always. So when you pray in tongues, you can be confident you are praying a prayer that will bring results.

When we pray in our native language, we may think we are praying the perfect prayer over our finances or our children or our careers. But sometimes—although we are praying with emotion—we are not praying accurately in accordance to how God wants to work things out for us.

When we acknowledge our weakness and yield our tongue in prayer to the Spirit over specific issues, we can know we are praying God's perfect will.

Indeed, when you let the Holy Spirit help you pray, you will surely tap into the First John 5:14-15 promise: "This is the confidence that we have in Him, that if we ask anything according to His will, He hears us. So if we know that He hears whatever we ask, we know that we have whatever we asked of Him" (MEV).

Finally, *The Passion Translation* goes even deeper, "God, the searcher of the heart, knows fully our longings, yet he also understands the desires of the Spirit, because the Holy Spirit passionately pleads before God for us, his holy ones, in perfect harmony with God's plan and our destiny."

Prayer

Father, in the name of Jesus, remind me to yield my tongue to Your Spirit when I am not certain what Your perfect will is—or when I am not getting prayer answers to situations I know You want to solve. Remind me to lift up my need to You through the gift of tongues.

Tapping into Supernatural Power

Jesus didn't leave us as orphans in the earth. When He ascended He said we would receive the promise of the Father—another comforter, the Holy Spirit. Jesus left record of this promise in Acts 1:8, "But you shall receive power when the Holy Spirit comes upon you. And you shall be My witnesses in Jerusalem, and in all Judea and Samaria, and to the ends of the earth" (MEV).

Now, the power is for more than witnessing to the resurrection of Christ. This supernatural power is for walking through trials, tribulations, and persecutions. This power is to combat the power of the enemy that comes against us at strategic times.

The Greek word for *power* in Acts 1:8 is *dunamis*. It's where we get the English word *dynamite*. Think about this: You have dynamite, explosive power on the inside of you waiting to be released through you. The Spirit who raised Christ from the dead lives in you! That's mind-blowing!

Think about it for a minute. Christ really died on that cross. He was really dead. He was really buried. But the Holy Spirit's power raised Him up from the grave on the third day. That same power is working in you and through you. When you pray in tongues, you tap directly into that power.

Let's go deeper into this definition. *The King James New Testament Greek Lexicon* defines *dunamis* as "strength, power, ability; inherent power, power residing in a thing by virtue of its nature, or which a person or thing exerts and puts forth; power for performing miracles; moral power and excellence of soul; the power and influence which belong to riches and wealth; and power consisting in or resting upon armies, forces, hosts." That's power!

I want you to understand this power within you. Meditate on this verse. The Amplified Classic translation puts Acts 1:8 this way: "But you shall receive power (ability, efficiency, and might) when the Holy Spirit has come upon you, and you shall be My witnesses in Jerusalem and all Judea and Samaria and to the ends (the very bounds) of the earth."

The Passion Translation puts it this way: "But I promise you this— the Holy Spirit will come upon you, and you will be seized with power. You will be my messengers to Jerusalem, throughout Judea, the distant provinces—even to the remotest places on earth!"

When you pray in tongues, you will find abilities and efficiencies. You will overcome instead of being overwhelmed. When you pray in tongues, you supercharge your spirit. Right about now is when you should cry out, "Holy Spirit, come upon me. Fill me again!"

Prayer

Father, in the name of Jesus, fill me again with Your Spirit. Give me a deep, lasting revelation of the power of God that dwells on the inside of me and an unction to live, move, have my being, pray, and prophesy in that dynamite power. When I am weak, lead me to pray in tongues to tap into Your strength.

Activating Your Spiritual Gifts

God gives you spiritual gifts and natural talents in line with your purpose. You can look at them as tools to get your assignment done. According to First Corinthians 12:7, each of us has at least one spiritual gift. Many people have more. God gives us what we need when we need it.

And we are exhorted in First Peter 4:10: "As each one has received a gift, minister it to one another, as good stewards of the manifold grace of God." We see an explanation of the nine gifts of the Spirit in First Corinthians 12:4-11. Paul wrote:

> *There are diversities of gifts, but the same Spirit. There are differences of ministries, but the same Lord. And there are diversities of activities, but it is the same God who works all in all. But the manifestation of the Spirit is given to each one for the profit of all: for to one is given the word of wisdom through the Spirit, to another the word of knowledge through the same Spirit, to another faith by the same Spirit, to another gifts of healings by the same Spirit, to another the working of miracles, to another prophecy, to another discerning of spirits, to another different kinds of tongues, to another the interpretation of tongues. But one and the same Spirit works all these things, distributing to each one individually as He wills.*

Many times the Holy Spirit wants to manifest His gifts through us, but we are not sensitive enough to discern His unction. Sometimes that's because we're not fully activated in our gift. We received an impartation but did not step into activation.

Activation is different from impartation. Impartation is receiving something. Activation is turning on one's spiritual gifts through exercise or release. Activation comes from a charge. Jesus activated the disciples in their impartation in Matthew 10:7-8: "As you go, preach, saying, 'The kingdom of heaven is at hand.' Heal the sick, cleanse the lepers, raise the dead, and cast out demons" (MEV).

Check out my series "Activating the 9 Gifts of the Spirit" at www .schoolofthespirit.tv to find teaching and activations of your spiritual gifts. In the meantime, you can ask the Holy Spirit to activate you as you pray in tongues. Here's how it works: Pray in tongues and then obey His prompting to prophesy or release His gifts the next time you feel His charge.

Prayer

Father, in the name of Jesus, activate in me the gifts You have distributed to me. Make me sensitive to Your Spirit so I can discern Your charge to release the giftings and anointings You have given me to serve people.

Face Down the Tempter

We're all tempted at times. Jesus was even tempted in the wilderness—but He did not sin. If we're honest, we sometimes fall for the enemy's temptation. But we don't have to if we pray in tongues when our flesh is trying to come into agreement with the tempter.

When you are struggling with temptation of any kind—from gossip to a bad confession to the most serious sins—ask the Holy Spirit to help you. He is your helper. He's right there waiting for you to ask, and we even find scriptural backing for the Holy Spirit's rescuing power in the face of temptations.

Jesus connected prayer with the ability to overcome temptation. He told His disciples, "Watch and pray, lest you enter into temptation. The spirit indeed is willing, but the flesh is weak" (Matt. 26:41). Of course, you can pray the line from the Lord's Prayer, "Lead me not into temptation" (see Matt. 6:13). But you can also pray in tongues. It's kind of hard to sin—to overeat, to cuss, to speak idle words, and so on—when you are praying in tongues.

Paul assured the believers in Corinth, "No temptation has overtaken you except such as is common to man; but God is faithful, who will not allow you to be tempted beyond what you are able, but with the temptation will also make the way of escape, that you may be able to bear it" (1 Cor. 10:13).

I know from experience that praying in tongues helps us resist temptations. Praying in tongues strengthens our resolve in the face of the enemy's appeals to lead us into sin. The Holy Spirit counters the enemy's enticement by leading us into truth and holiness when we pray in tongues. When we pray in tongues much, we will be more sensitive to the Spirit's conviction when we do sin so that we don't walk in that state.

Romans 8:13 says, "For if you live according to the flesh, you will die, but if through the Spirit you put to death the deeds of the body, you will live" (MEV). The Bible speaks of the works of the flesh, which are many. The works of the flesh include "adultery, fornication, uncleanness, lewdness, idolatry, sorcery, hatred, contentions, jealousies, outbursts of wrath, selfish ambitions, dissensions, heresies, envy, murders, drunkenness, revelries, and the like; of which I tell you beforehand, just as I also told you in time past, that those who practice such things will not inherit the kingdom of God" (Gal. 5:19-21).

Our flesh wars against the Spirit and the Spirit wars against the flesh (see Gal. 5:17) When we pray in tongues, we are agreeing with the Spirit and can overcome our flesh. Galatians 5:16 puts it this way: "I say then, walk in the Spirit, and you shall not fulfill the lust of the flesh" (MEV). If you pray in tongues, you are more likely to walk in the Spirit instead of the flesh.

Prayer

Father, in the name of Jesus, would You remind me to begin praying in tongues at the first tempting thought? Help me remember to yield my voice to Your utterance so You can empower me to face down the tempter.

BENEFIT 9

Unlock Glorious Truth

Jesus is the way, the truth and the life (see John 14:6). Jesus told Pilate He came to testify to the truth, and everyone who loves truth recognizes His voice (see John 18:37). Jesus was the Word made flesh, and the Word is truth (see John 17:17).

Of course, Jesus doesn't walk with us on the earth as He did with His disciples over two thousand years go. The Holy Spirit took His place as the truth giver in the earth. The Holy Spirit is known by the name Spirit of Truth. Jesus told His disciples:

> I still have many things to say to you, but you cannot bear them now. However, when He, the Spirit of truth, has come, He will guide you into all truth; for He will not speak on His own authority, but whatever He hears He will speak; and He will tell you things to come. He will glorify Me, for He will take of what is Mine and declare it to you (John 16:12-14).

The Spirit of Truth has been around since the beginning and dwells on the inside of us. We are the temple of the Spirit of Truth. One of the Holy Spirit's job descriptions is to guide you into all truth. Other translations say "lead you into all truth" or "teach you all truth" or "reveal the truth." Are you getting the idea?

When you pray in tongues, you are unlocking glorious truths about God, His Kingdom, His ways, His principles, and so on. Praying in tongues leads you, guides you, teaches you, and reveals to you the truth you need to know when you need to know it. Praying in tongues is critical to tapping into the truth for your life in any given situation. It's a key to tapping into the truth that sets you free from the enemy's lies or wrong teachings you've digested.

Praying in tongues makes us aware of the truth about ourselves that we need to see so we can change, the truth about others for better or worse, the truth about circumstances so we are not led astray. Praying in tongues helps you worship God in spirit and in truth (see John 4:24). When you pray in tongues, you are calling on Him in truth (see Ps. 145:18).

The Lord is not trying to hide the truth from you. Sometimes God doesn't disclose certain truths to you because you do not yet need to know them or you aren't ready to receive them. But if there is a truth you need to know, Jesus is not trying to hide that present-day truth you need to walk in victory.

In this day and age we need to treasure the truth more than silver and gold. Deception is rising rampantly in the world and in the church. We need to stick close to the Holy Ghost and ask Him to do what Jesus promises He will do—reveal the truth. Ask the Holy Spirit the truth about your marriage, the Scriptures, the future—or any other area— then pray in tongues. He is faithful to reveal truth.

Prayer

Father, in the name of Jesus, would You reveal the truth I need to know as I pray in tongues. Lead me, guide me, teach me truth as I pray with the help of Your Holy Spirit. I want to be a lover of the truth.

Always Have the Right Words to Say

I've had more than a few crucial conversations in life. Sometimes, I just had no idea what to say. I was afraid to say the wrong thing and make things worse, but I knew I had to say something.

Thankfully, I've learned praying in tongues helps me find the right words to say in difficult situations. And you can count on the same results when you pray in tongues over an issue where natural words elude you.

Jesus said, "Now when they bring you to the synagogues and magistrates and authorities, do not worry about how or what you should answer, or what you should say. For the Holy Spirit will teach you in that very hour what you ought to say" (Luke 12:11-12).

You are not likely to be dragged before authorities in this context—though you may be pulled over by a cop or face a lawsuit—but you can apply this promise to difficult situations in which you need to find the right words to say.

The Passion Translation puts it this way: "And remember this: When people publicly accuse you and forcefully drag you before the religious leaders and authorities, do not be troubled. Don't worry about defending yourself or how to answer their accusations. Simply be confident and allow the Spirit of Wisdom access to your heart, and in that very moment he will reveal what you are to say to them."

This is an anxiety-reducing promise! Many times, God does not give us the wisdom we need until the very moment we need it. But if we pray in tongues over the situation we can be confident God will put the right words in our mouth when we have to face the people involved. Praying in tongues prepares you for unpleasant conversations and confrontations.

The Message translation offers this: "When they drag you into their meeting places, or into police courts and before judges, don't worry about defending yourselves—what you'll say or how you'll say it. The right words will be there. The Holy Spirit will give you the right words when the time comes."

That means we don't have to get into imaginations and play out the confrontational conversations in our head. We just have to trust the Holy Spirit that He will supernaturally put words of wisdom in our mouth because we intentionally yielded our tongue to His utterance in prayer.

And here's some more good news: Even if you don't have time to pray right before the conversation, He can put the very words in your mouth in an instant when you cultivate the discipline to pray in tongues.

Prayer

Father, in the name of Jesus, help me discipline myself to pray in tongues when my mind doesn't know what to say. Prepare my heart to receive Your words and speak them through my mouth in the right moment. As I open my mouth, Lord, fill it with the right words.

BENEFIT 11

Strengthen
Your Physical Body

When I was doing missions work in Nicaragua in 100-degree weather for 18 hours a day—day after day—my body was dehydrated and worn out. I had to quickly learn that God's grace was available to do what He called me to do, and I could tap into that grace through praying in tongues.

Paul explained this process in Romans 8:11: "But if the Spirit of Him who raised Jesus from the dead lives in you, He who raised Christ from the dead will also give life to your mortal bodies through His Spirit that lives in you" (MEV).

Think about it for a minute. If the Holy Spirit can give life to our dead bodies in the resurrection when Jesus cracks the sky, don't you think His life in us can strengthen our weary bodies while we do His will on earth? That same spirit that resurrected Christ and that will resurrect us at the Second Coming can strengthen us while we walk through physically challenging tasks on the earth. One way He does this is through praying in tongues.

The Amplified Classic translation says, "And if the Spirit of Him Who raised up Jesus from the dead dwells in you, [then] He Who raised up Christ Jesus from the dead will also restore to life your mortal (short-lived, perishable) bodies through His Spirit Who dwells in you."

Although this is speaking of restoration of life after we die in Christ, the same principle applies to our current life as we live and move and have our being in Christ (see Acts 17:28). Praying in tongues helps us tap into that life-giving power to sustain us when life's demands take a toll on our physical bodies.

When I pray in tongues, it energizes me. I can be exhausted, but when I give my tongue over the Holy Spirit's utterance it sets a fire under me. My batteries are recharged. I used to try to pray in tongues while I was going to sleep, but I discovered I could not go to sleep because it energized me.

Paul shared, "Therefore we do not lose heart. Even though our outward man is perishing, yet the inward man is being renewed day by day" (2 Cor. 4:16). Eventually, our physical body decays, but our spirit sustains us through difficult physical issues as we pray in tongues. In fact, Proverbs 18:14 tells us, "The spirit of a man will sustain him in sickness."

Think about that! Resurrection life is on the inside of you. We need to put our faith on the reality that praying in tongues strengthens our mortal bodies to run our race and fight the good fight of faith even when our bodies are exhausted.

Prayer

Father, in the name of Jesus, give me the revelation of how Your Spirit can sustain my body in times of stress and trial and warfare. When I walk through fire and water and my body wants to give in, help me pray in tongues and walk in power.

BENEFIT 12

Your Secret Prayer Life

P raying in tongues is like a covert prayer operation. When you pray in tongues, you are praying secret prayers between you and God and the enemy is absolutely dumbfounded. You may not understand a word you are saying, but that's okay because God does—and the enemy doesn't. The enemy can't hinder your tongues prayers because he's absolutely clueless as to what you and God are up to.

Paul wrote, "For he who speaks in a tongue does not speak to men but to God, for no one understands him" (1 Cor. 14:2). Again, that no one includes the enemy. If you pray out loud the enemy can hear you. It's not satan himself listening in to your prayers, but monitoring spirits watch, listen, and report back to demonic networks that have allied against you.

Consider this: When the enemy hears your prayers, you may think you are getting confirmation about important decisions, but the enemy may be arranging circumstances to deceive you. Or, the enemy will try to delay and hinder your prayers answers like he did to the prophet Daniel.

You might say, "Well, I'll just pray in my head and the enemy won't hear me." True, but you may not be praying the perfect prayer. Romans 8:26 tells us we don't know how to pray as we ought. There's nothing wrong with praying in your head, but why not also pray in tongues so you release secret, perfect prayer? That's what Paul did. He prayed in his natural language and he prayed in tongues (see 1 Cor. 14:15).

The Amplified Classic translation says, "For one who speaks in an [unknown] tongue speaks not to men but to God, for no one understands or catches his meaning." This is stealth prayer. Yes, the enemy can hear you pray in tongues, and he may try to oppose you in various areas, but at least he doesn't have the particulars of the prayers for God's perfect will that your tongues release.

The New Living Translation tells us, "For if you have the ability to speak in tongues, you will be talking only to God, since people won't be able to understand you." And the Contemporary English Version says, "If you speak languages that others don't know, God will understand what you are saying, though no one else will know what you mean."

I met a woman in Alabama once and she fancied a gentleman. She did not pray about it out loud because she didn't want the enemy to interfere with the relationship. Then again, sometimes we enter the wrong relationship. I believe we would have less resistance from the enemy over God's will for our life if we prayed in tongues more because by the time he figures out what we prayed, God's will has already manifested.

Prayer

Father, in the name of Jesus, help me not to be quick to speak out in prayer about issues that might draw the enemy's attention. Give me wisdom to know when praying in tongues is the best option for seeing Your will come to pass in my life with the least resistance.

Access the Mysteries of God

When I was doing missions work in Nicaragua—part of which was videography and producing documentaries—one of the pastors on the trip called me over to sit down with him in the white plastic chairs around the compound. I was glad to, given the scorching heat and the heavy camera bags.

When I sat down, he didn't say hello. He didn't ask me how I was doing. He looked me dead in the eye and he recited First Corinthians 14:2, "For he who speaks in a tongue does not speak to men but to God, for no one understands him; however, in the spirit he speaks mysteries."

That's all he said. He just returned to praying in tongues. I knew what he meant. I knew he was giving me a key to access the mysteries of God. From that moment on, I started praying in tongues as much as I possibly could and, lo and behold, I started accessing the mysteries of God.

Now, when you think of mysteries you may think of the popular game Clue, Sue Grafton novels, or Sherlock Holmes. But I'm talking about the mysteries of the Kingdom of heaven. Mysteries are truths that are beyond our understanding without revelation. They are spiritual secrets.

The Good News Translation of First Corinthians 14:2 translates the verse like this: "They are speaking secret truths by the power of the Spirit." Jesus told His disciples—and this applies to us—"It has been given to you to know the mysteries of the kingdom of heaven" (Matt. 13:11). Knowledge of mysteries is part of your spiritual inheritance.

In his book *The Glory Within*, Corey Russell describes the Holy Spirit as the search engine of heaven. Think about how you Google something on the web to find answers to things you don't know. Maybe you don't know how to cook a pot roast. You can Google it and unlock that mystery. When you pray in tongues, you can discover mysteries of the Kingdom.

What are these mysteries? I write more about mysteries in my book *The Seer Dimensions*, but here are a few: There's the mystery of the gospel (see Eph. 6:19); the mystery of Christ (see Col. 4:3); the mystery of iniquity (see 2 Thess. 2:7); the mystery of faith (see 1 Tim. 3:9); the mystery of godliness (see 1 Tim. 3:16); the mystery of the seven stars (see Rev. 1:20).

There are many ways to access the mysteries of the Kingdom of heaven. They are hidden in the Word. The Holy Spirit can share them with you by direct revelation. You can discover them through teachings from leaders in the Body of Christ and so on. But praying in tongues is one of the fastest ways to access these mysteries.

Prayer

Father, in the name of Jesus, would You give me a hunger to search out secret truths and mysteries of Your Kingdom so I can understand You ways. As I pray in tongues, would You unlock deep mysteries of Your glory?

Fortify Your Spiritual Armor

God's armor can't be penetrated—or even dented. The only way you can get hit by the fiery dart is if you don't armor up—or if you don't lift up your shield of faith. But you can strengthen your faith and thereby fortify your spiritual armor while you pray in tongues.

When I pray in tongues in the middle of the battle, it seems like my sword is a little sharper. It's as if the Holy Spirit is helping us lift up the shield of faith and helping us swing His sword. Paul explained in Ephesians 6:12-13:

> *For we do not wrestle against flesh and blood, but against principalities, against powers, against the rulers of the darkness of this age, against spiritual hosts of wickedness in the heavenly places. Therefore take up the whole armor of God, that you may be able to withstand in the evil day, and having done all, to stand.*

After Paul described the demonic hierarchy, he used the word *therefore*. When you see *therefore* in Scripture, you have to ask what is the "therefore" there for. In this case, Paul was teaching us why we needed the whole armor. Praying in tongues fortifies our spiritual armor. Paul continues in Ephesians 6:14-18:

Stand therefore, having girded your waist with truth, having put on the breastplate of righteousness, and having shod your feet with the preparation of the gospel of peace; above all, taking the shield of faith with which you will be able to quench all the fiery darts of the wicked one. And take the helmet of salvation, and the sword of the Spirit, which is the word of God; praying always with all prayer and supplication in the Spirit, being watchful to this end with all perseverance and supplication for all the saints.

In some seasons of heavy spiritual warfare, I will engage in a prophetic act and actually symbolically put on each piece of God's armor Paul described, one by one. I also pray in tongues because of what Paul stressed in Ephesians 6:18: "Praying always with all prayer and supplication in the Spirit." *The Passion Translation* says, "pray passionately in the Spirit." Basically Paul is saying, "Put on all this armor and pray while you do it." There are many ways to pray, but praying in tongues fortifies our spiritual armor.

Prayer

Father, in the name of Jesus, remind me to put on my whole armor of God before I enter the battlefield. Give me an unction to pray in tongues as I get dressed for the war You are leading me into. I know victory is my portion.

BENEFIT 15

Cultivate the Fruit
of the Spirit

When the Holy Spirit came to dwell on the inside of you, He brought all of His fruit with Him in seed form. Of course, you and I both know that we have to activate—or cultivate—that fruit. We can cultivate the fruit of the Spirit in our lives by yielding our tongue to the Holy Spirit's utterance.

Paul outlines the fruit of the Spirit in Galatians 5:22-23, "But the fruit of the Spirit is love, joy, peace, longsuffering, kindness, goodness, faithfulness, gentleness, self-control. Against such there is no law."

Aren't you glad there's no law against joy and peace and so on? Even unbelievers appreciate someone who carries the fruit of the Spirit and, indeed, displaying that fruit for the world to see makes Christ more attractive to them. Cultivating the fruit of the Spirit makes us better witnesses to the love of God.

The Passion Translation puts it this way, "But the fruit produced by the Holy Spirit within you is divine love in all its varied expressions: joy that overflows, peace that subdues, patience that endures, kindness in action, a life full of virtue, faith that prevails, gentleness of heart, and strength of spirit. Never set the law above these qualities, for they are meant to be limitless."

When we pray in tongues with the intention of cultivating His fruit in our hearts, He is agreeing with the Father's will to see us walk in joy that overflows, peace that subdues, patience that endures, kindness in action, a life full of virtue, faith that prevails, gentleness of heart, and strength of spirit. Meditate on that as you pray in tongues and watch the fruit of the Spirit grow in your life.

The Amplified Classic version says:

> *But the fruit of the [Holy] Spirit [the work which His presence within accomplishes] is love, joy (gladness), peace, patience (an even temper, forbearance), kindness, goodness (benevolence), faithfulness, gentleness (meekness, humility), self-control (self-restraint, continence). Against such things there is no law [that can bring a charge].*

Praying in tongues waters the seed of the fruit of the Spirit that the Holy Ghost brought with Him when He came to live on the inside of you. Praying in tongues is like watering your grass. If you want healthy grass, you have to turn on the sprinklers—and you have to pull weeds. Praying in tongues waters the Seed of the fruit and gets rid of the weeds at the same time!

Prayer

Father, in name of Jesus, I want to cultivate Your glorious fruit in my life so I can enjoy my life, walk deeply in love, and point others to Christ. As I pray in tongues, would You water the seeds of Your fruit within me?

Mortify Your Flesh

You've heard of crucifying your flesh. But the Bible also speaks of mortifying the flesh as another level of putting down your carnal nature. If you haven't read the King James Version of the Bible, you probably aren't familiar with the verse in Romans 8:13, "For if ye live after the flesh, ye shall die: but if ye through the Spirit do mortify the deeds of the body, ye shall live."

Mortify means "to subdue or deaden (the body, bodily appetites, etc.) especially by abstinence or self-inflicted pain or discomfort; to destroy the strength, vitality, or functioning of." Sounds intense, doesn't it? When we pray in tongues with a heart to mortify our flesh, the Holy Spirit can choose to speed up the process. We need His help because our flesh never agrees with God. Paul wrote:

> *The sinful nature wants to do evil, which is just the opposite of what the Spirit wants. And the Spirit gives us desires that are the opposite of what the sinful nature desires. These two forces are constantly fighting each other, so you are not free to carry out your good intentions* (Galatians 5:17 NLT).

We all have a sinful nature to contend with. Adam and Eve were created sinless, but they disobeyed God's command not to eat from the Tree of the Knowledge of Good and Evil. Thanks be to God, He sent Jesus Christ to free us from sin and death. But we must agree in our spirits and our souls against our flesh and choose to enter into mortification in the areas we see are weak spots.

For example, if you have a fleshly habit you can't kick with willpower, praying in tongues can help you overcome it. Paul said he disciplined his body and made it his servant (see 1 Cor. 9:27). I don't believe he depended on willpower alone, but on the power of the Holy Spirit through praying in tongues. When you put your will with His will in prayer, you will see results.

Paul advised the church at Colossae, "Therefore put to death your members which are on the earth: fornication, uncleanness, passion, evil desire, and covetousness, which is idolatry" (Col. 3:5). When you pray in tongues, the Holy Spirit may start showing you things and even wrestling with you over some sinful habits, but He just wants your agreement. He wants you to repent.

If the Holy Spirit is wrestling with you, let Him win. When you surrender to the will of the Holy Spirit and trust Him to pray the perfect mortification prayer through you, you will see faster and lasting results than you could accomplish in your own strength alone.

Prayer

Father, in the name of Jesus, give me the courage to mortify my flesh as I pray in tongues. Help me to agree with what You want to deal with in my life and trust You to do the mortification work in me that my spirit craves but my flesh hates.

Moved by
Holy Spirit's Impulses

P aul makes it clear: "For all who are led by the Spirit of God are sons of God" (Rom. 8:14 AMPC). This is a familiar verse to many, but I love how *The Passion Translation* puts this: "moved by the impulses of the Holy Spirit." *The Message* translation puts it this way: "God's Spirit beckons. There are things to do and places to go!"

That is our goal as believers in the Lord Jesus Christ. We want to live and move and have our being in Him (see Acts 17:28). Praying in tongues absolutely helps you to better sense the Holy Spirit's leading. You will pick up on His sudden, spontaneous inclinations to do or say something—or not do or say something.

Sometimes we find ourselves with those inclinations without even realizing it is the Holy Spirit moving us. The more you pray in tongues, the more this sudden leading and flashes of inspiration will become part of your spiritual life.

Paul was called to preach the gospel to the Gentiles, and he got about his Father's business with as much zeal as he formerly displayed in persecuting the church. Paul traveled the world over in his day, but when he and his apostolic team went through certain cities to preach the Word the Holy Spirit stopped him in favor of a more strategic mission. In Acts 16:6-10, Luke records:

> *Now when they had gone through Phrygia and the region of Galatia, they were forbidden by the Holy Spirit to preach the*

word in Asia. After they had come to Mysia, they tried to go into Bithynia, but the Spirit did not permit them. So passing by Mysia, they came down to Troas. And a vision appeared to Paul in the night. A man of Macedonia stood and pleaded with him, saying, "Come over to Macedonia and help us." Now after he had seen the vision, immediately we sought to go to Macedonia, concluding that the Lord had called us to preach the gospel to them.

Paul concluded that the Lord wanted him to preach the gospel in Macedonia only after the Holy Spirit twice prevented him from preaching in other cities, then gave him a vision that clearly laid out the next leg of his missionary journey. In other words, Paul had his plans, but the Holy Spirit had different plans. Paul could have mistakenly blamed the devil for the obstacles to getting the gospel out in Phyrgia and the region of Galatia and Bithynia, but he discerned it was the Holy Spirit—not the devil—preventing him from fulfilling his mission.

None of us are led by the Spirit perfectly, but we can get better and better and better at it. Praying in tongues helps us tune into the Holy Spirit's leadership in every area of our life.

Prayer

Father, in the name of Jesus, I want to submit fully to Your leadership. I want to tune into Your impulses. As I pray in tongues, would You make me more sensitive to Your spontaneous, sudden inclinations?

Accelerate Your Spiritual Growth

When we're children, we grow without trying. It's an automatic process. That's not so in the realm of the Spirit. We have to sow to the Spirit if we want to grow in the Spirit. Praying in tongues accelerates our spiritual growth, which is critical to walking in consistent victory.

But accelerating our spiritual growth is not just for our benefit—it's for the benefit of the Kingdom. When we grow we can flow more accurately with the Holy Spirit and tap into our highest calling and be a strong example of the Holy Spirit's transforming work in our lives.

Paul made it plain: "The Spirit Himself bears witness with our spirit that we are children of God" (Rom. 8:16). We start our walk as babes in Christ, then we mature into children, but eventually we reach spiritual adulthood. One of my goals is to accelerate that maturation process by sowing to the Spirit.

Think about it for a minute: Sonship denotes a greater level of maturity than a child. When you have a child, you give them small tasks. Grown sons have the strength to take on greater responsibilities. You may let your little child sit on your lap and play with the steering wheel of your car. But you would give your grown son the keys to go to the store and pick up supplies.

Paul told us, "For the earnest expectation of the creation eagerly waits for the revealing of the sons of God" (Rom. 8:19). This is what the whole earth is waiting on. A child can only complete so much of God's will. A mature son can do more for the Father than a child.

We grow in maturity from a child to a son, which is why the earth is waiting for the revealing. Other translations say the manifestation of the sons of God. Sons are equipped and prepared to do the greater works. Praying in tongues helps us mature from children to sons.

Again, Paul said, "For all who are led by the Spirit of God are sons of God" (Rom. 8:14 AMPC). The Christian Standard Bible puts it this way: "For all those led by God's Spirit are God's sons." Again, there's a difference in Scripture between children of God and sons of God. Sons are those who are mature. Children need to be pampered. Sons receive the inheritance.

Ephesians 4:13 shows us we have some growing up to do: "till we all come to the unity of the faith and of the knowledge of the Son of God, to a perfect man, to the measure of the stature of the fullness of Christ." Praying in tongues helps us mature from children to sons—and accelerates that maturity.

Prayer

Father, in the name of Jesus, would You help accelerate my spiritual growth as I pray in tongues? Help me set aside childish things and move more deeply into the Spirit-led life You've called me to live.

Walk Accurately
in the Spirit

Although we're all born again, we still have a free will. We can choose to walk in the flesh or walk in the Spirit. When we walk in the flesh, we reap destruction, but when we walk in the Spirit we will reap everlasting life (see Gal. 6:8).

We don't want to be carnal Christians. We want to walk accurately in the Spirit. Galatians 5:16 tells us, "Walk in the Spirit, and you shall not fulfill the lust of the flesh." The flesh is connected with a body of sin. And the wages of sin is death (see Rom. 6:23). Praying in tongues helps you walk accurately in the Spirit.

The Passion Translation of Galatians 5:16 offers richer language to describe these realities: "As you yield to the dynamic life and power of the Holy Spirit, you will abandon the cravings of your self-life."

That means you follow the Holy Spirit because your will is aligned with His will. You fully submit and surrender to His leadership with one-hundredfold obedience because your spirit wants what His Spirit wants and you reject the lusts of the flesh and the resistance in your soul. That happens as you pray in tongues.

The Message translation offers, "My counsel is this: Live freely, animated and motivated by God's Spirit." Praying in tongues helps you walk accurately in the Spirit. You won't want anything to do with the flesh. You won't want anything to do with the soulish inclinations. You will reject self-will and fully and freely embrace God's will.

Walking in the Spirit has a practical meaning. God is a practical Father. Jesus is a practical Savior. The Holy Spirit is a practical Helper. Practically, when you pray in tongues you will learn to live your life walking in the precepts of the Spirit. One step at a time, day by day, you walk in His will and His ways as He leads you and guides you. You yield to Him and do things His way, because His way is the best way.

Finally, the Amplified Classic version gives us some additional insight: "But I say, walk and live [habitually] in the [Holy] Spirit [responsive to and controlled and guided by the Spirit]; then you will certainly not gratify the cravings and desires of the flesh (of human nature without God)."

Praying in tongues helps us live out this verse and see the associated benefits. We'd have a lot less trouble in life if we would walk in His way instead of our way. His ways are higher than our ways (see Isa. 55:8-9). When you walk accurately in the Spirit, you will be walking in His perfect plans and purposes and live your best life.

Prayer

Father, in the name of Jesus, I want to walk accurately in Your Sprit. As I pray in tongues today, would You do a work in me that helps me discern Your leadership at every turn? I will follow You.

Break Religious Mindsets

Nobody likes religious, legalistic Christians any more than Jesus appreciated the Pharisees in His day. Christians who carry religious mindsets minister death, condemnation, guilt, and shame.

Of course, we can also be legalistic toward ourselves and make ourselves miserable. Often, we are exposed to legalistic mindsets before we come to know the Lord. You don't have to be saved to be legalistic. Others grow up in churches steeped in religion that put more laws down than Moses—laws we can never live up to.

Praying in tongues helps you break off and break through religious mindsets that prevent you from experiencing the deep liberty and joy the Holy Spirit has to offer. Praying in tongues shifts you from legalism to life.

In Second Corinthians 3:6 Paul wrote this speaking of Christ: "who also made us sufficient as ministers of the new covenant, not of the letter but of the Spirit; for the letter kills, but the Spirit gives life."

Jesus came to fulfill the law. Although the Ten Commandments are still valid and vital to our lives today, the Pharisees had prescribed another ten thousand man-made laws that no one was capable of keeping. That's why we needed the Christ, the sinless Lamb of God. He paid the price for our perfection, and He is not legalistic.

Paul put it this way, "There is therefore now no condemnation to those who are in Christ Jesus, who do not walk according to the flesh, but according to the Spirit" (Rom. 8:1). Legalism condemns. Praying in tongues helps you avoid religious, legalistic mindsets.

Paul wrote, "But if you are led by the Spirit, you are not under the law" (Gal. 5:18). Sometimes, even the best of us want to hold people to the letter of the law with man-made traditions and rules. Jesus gave us one new commandment: "'You shall love the Lord your God with all your heart, with all your soul, with all your strength, and with all your mind,' and 'your neighbor as yourself'" (Luke 10:27). That is the new law.

The Amplified Classic version translates Galatians 5:18 this way: "But if you are guided (led) by the [Holy] Spirit, you are not subject to the Law." That doesn't mean we're lawless, it means we are subject to the law of liberty rather than in bondage and in the fear of punishment (see James 2:12). Praying in tongues helps you avoid religious mindsets.

The New Living Translation says, "But when you are directed by the Spirit, you are not under obligation to the law of Moses." And *The Passion Translation* notes: "But when you yield to the life of the Spirit, you will no longer be living under the law, but soaring above it!"

When you pray in tongues, you will stop looking at things from a legalistic, religious, law mindset. You will begin to look at things from a perspective of grace and liberty as the Holy Spirit roots that religious mindset out of you.

Prayer

Father, in the name of Jesus, I don't want to live with a legalistic mindset—condemning myself and others for not living a perfect life. As I pray in tongues, would You root the religious spirit out of my mind? Would You free me from legalistic attitudes?

Develop Sensitivity to Spiritual Things

Praying in tongues makes you more sensitive to spiritual things. That's because when you pray in tongues you are shutting off your natural mind and setting your mind on spiritual things. And we know when we sow to the Spirit, we reap from the Spirit.

Paul explains this concept in Romans 8:5, "For those who live according to the flesh set their minds on the things of the flesh, but those who live according to the Spirit, the things of the Spirit."

When you set your mind on the flesh, you will gratify the flesh. When you set your mind on eating a hamburger after church, you will probably go eat a hamburger after church.

The New Living Translation puts it this way: "Those who are dominated by the sinful nature think about sinful things, but those who are controlled by the Holy Spirit think about things that please the Spirit."

Where the mind goes, the man follows. If your main concern in life is catering to your physical needs then you are going to living according to the demands of the flesh. Paul said he buffeted his body (see 1 Cor. 9:27). That's King James Version for *discipline my body*—or to bring it under control. Paul wasn't led by his flesh, in part, because he prayed in tongues so much.

Next time you go out to dinner, listen to the conversations of the staff or the other diners. They are speaking about secular, worldly desires and activities. They are talking about partying or greedy ambition. Their mind is set on fleshly things. The sad thing is, some Christians have similar conversations. We want to set our minds on the things of the Spirit. One way we do that is by praying in tongues.

The Passion Translation emphasizes this concept: "Those who are motivated by the flesh only pursue what benefits themselves. But those who live by the impulses of the Holy Spirit are motivated to pursue spiritual realities."

If you want to be more sensitive to spiritual things, pray in tongues. You are intentionally aligning yourself with an activity that will make you more sensitive to the spiritual realm. We want to acknowledge the God who dwells in us, not just the Father who sits on the throne in heaven and the Jesus who sits at the right hand of the Father.

The Message offers: "Those who trust God's action in them find that God's Spirit is in them—living and breathing God! Obsession with self in these matters is a dead end; attention to God leads us out into the open, into a spacious, free life."

If you want to be more successful in life, set your mind on things above more than you set your mind on the things of the earth. As you pray in tongues more and more, you will trust God's action in you.

Prayer

Father, in the name of Jesus, would You help me to keep my mind on spiritual things rather than letting the spirit of the world renew my mind to fleshly ventures? As I pray in tongues, open my heart to spiritual realities.

Understand Spiritual Truths

When we pray in tongues, we are positioning ourselves to understand spiritual truths—the deeper things of God that inform our journey and intimacy with Him. Paul explained, "These things we also speak, not in words which man's wisdom teaches but which the Holy Spirit teaches, comparing spiritual things with spiritual" (1 Cor. 2:13).

Paul taught by the spirit and those who had spiritual ears understood his message. Spiritual truths don't make any sense to the natural mind. The Holy Spirit, our Teacher, has to help us understand. The Holy Spirit leads us and guides us into all truth (see John 16:13)—and that includes spiritual truths and how to apply them to our everyday lives.

At first glance, it can be difficult to understand some of what we read in the Bible—and there are often layers of meaning. Some of the spiritual truths in scripture come in the form of proverbs, dark sayings, dreams, visions, and parables.

Before I was a Christian, I went to a Christian university. I had to write papers on books of the Bible, and I completed the work but had no spiritual understanding about what I was reading. Mentally, I was able to find the patterns and trends as if I was reading history. But I had no spiritual insight. In Mark 4:10-12, Jesus quoted from Isaiah 6:9-10:

> *But when He was alone, those around Him with the twelve asked Him about the parable. And He said to them, "To you it has been given to know the mystery of the kingdom of God;*

but to those who are outside, all things come in parables, so that 'Seeing they may see and not perceive, and hearing they may hear and not understand; lest they should turn, and their sins be forgiven them.'"

The Pharisees rejected Jesus and the Holy Spirit, so they could not understand spiritual truths. When you pray in tongues, you are leaning into the Spirit of truth and the truth becomes more accessible and understandable over time.

The Amplified Classic translation of First Corinthians 2:13 reads: "And we are setting these truths forth in words not taught by human wisdom but taught by the [Holy] Spirit, combining and interpreting spiritual truths with spiritual language [to those who possess the Holy Spirit]."

Praying in tongues gives us a greater propensity to understand spiritual truths. Raising people from the dead, for example, doesn't make any natural sense to the medical world, but it makes perfect sense in the Kingdom. This is a deep spiritual truth we can hang our faith on to fulfill Christ's command to heal the sick and raise the dead. How man can speak for God through prophecy makes no sense to the natural mind.

Finally, meditate on *The Passion Translation*'s rendition of this verse: "And we articulate these realities with the words imparted to us by the Spirit and not with the words taught by human wisdom. We join together Spirit-revealed truths with Spirit-revealed words."

Prayer

Father, in the name of Jesus, I want to discover spiritual truths in the Word and in the spirit dimensions. As I pray in tongues, would You open my eyes to deep spiritual truths that are relevant to my walk with You?

More Aware of the Father's Love

God is love—and He wants us to experience the depth and height and breadth and length of His unconditional love. He wants us to experience this in a way that surpasses head knowledge. So we can be filled to the measure of the fullness of God (see Eph. 3:19).

Too many believers have identity issues. They feel guilty, condemned, or ashamed. These emotions are not the will of God for our lives and actually may cause us to shut Him out—and shut people out.

Paul wrote these words, "Now hope does not disappoint, because the love of God has been poured out in our hearts by the Holy Spirit who was given to us" (Rom. 5:5). The New Living Translation puts it this way: "For we know how dearly God loves us, because he has given us the Holy Spirit to fill our hearts with his love."

Praying in tongues makes you more aware of—and more confident—of the Father's love. That revelation changes everything. Even if you don't feel the love of God, by faith you know He loves you. When storms come, you can stand on the revelation that God loves you, and if God loves you He will help you. *The Passion Translation* of Romans 5:5 says, "We can now experience the endless love of God cascading into our hearts through the Holy Spirit who lives in us!"

Praying in tongues breaks down the walls that keep us from experiencing the love of God. When people haven't loved us well, we may think we're unlovable. But God, who is love, died for us even when we were opposing His Kingdom. His love led us to repentance. And His love heals us.

Jesus gave us one new commandment in John 13:34-35: "A new command I give you: Love one another. As I have loved you, so you must love one another. By this everyone will know that you are my disciples, if you love one another" (NIV). Jesus also said, "'You shall love the Lord your God with all your heart, with all your soul, with all your strength, and with all your mind,' and 'your neighbor as yourself'" (Luke 10:27).

We can't love ourselves and others if we don't receive God's love. We can't love our neighbor or love God (which translates to obeying God) if we don't first receive the love of God. It takes God to love God. You can't love God unless you receive God's love first. We love Him because He first loved us (see 1 John 4:19).

Praying in tongues makes us more sensitive and aware of the Father's love. When we are aware of God's love for us, it will transform us. It will renew our minds. It will make our heart tender toward others. Praying in tongues revolutionizes our love walk.

Prayer

Father, in the name of Jesus, would You give me an awareness of Your great love for me? As I pray in tongues, break down any walls that my pain has built around my heart so I can experience Your love.

Taught to Do God's Will

The Holy Spirit is our Teacher. Sometimes we don't quite catch on to what He is teaching us about what the Father wants us to do. Praying in tongues teaches us to do God's will. We may not hear His voice telling us what to do, but we will be inspired with a revelation that leads us down the right path.

In Psalm 143:10, David cried out, "Teach me to do Your will, for You are my God; Your Spirit is good. Lead me in the land of uprightness." Of course, there's more than one way of learning or discerning God's will. But praying in tongues makes God's will clearer in our lives. It helps us to cut through the confusion over what God wants us to do in any given aspect of our lives, from marriage to career to church and beyond.

God is a good God, and He wants you to know His will. The Holy Spirit knows the perfect will of the Father. First Corinthians 2:11 tells us the Holy Spirit "knows the mind of God." The Holy Spirit knows all things—including the answers to your problems and how you should make decisions—because He is God. When you pray in tongues you are praying according to the will of God. The result is you will better discern His will.

The Message puts David's prayer this way: "Teach me how to live to please you, because you're my God. Lead me by your blessed Spirit into cleared and level pastureland." Many people are so confused about the will of God. They enter into the paralysis of analysis trying to figure out what to do.

Praying in tongues teaches us to do the will of God. Our natural mind will be enlightened with a revelation of the will of God. We will suddenly know what to do and be confident in that knowledge.

The Amplified Classic version translates Psalm 143:10 this way: "Teach me to do Your will, for You are my God; let Your good Spirit lead me into a level country and into the land of uprightness." Praying in tongues unlocks the revelation of God's will for our lives, which is critical.

Think about it. One wrong decision can derail your life for months or years. You can marry the wrong person and destroy your life for a decade. You can take the wrong job and sell yourself short.

The Passion Translation says: "So teach me, Lord, for you are my God. Your gracious Spirit is all I need, so lead me on good paths that are pleasing to you, my one and only God!" Praying in tongues positions you to have your mind enlightened to God's will. Pray in tongues about God's will for your life until you feel a peace. Then wait for the revelation.

Prayer

Father, in the name of Jesus, would You teach me to do Your will as I pray in tongues. Will You unlock the revelation of what You want me to do and how You want me to do it? I will follow You.

Unlocking Supernatural Favor

Because praying in tongues helps you cultivate the fruit of the Spirit, mortifies your flesh, and otherwise helps you walk in the Spirit, one byproduct is favor with God and man. If you have favor with God, He can give you favor with man.

Proverbs 16:7 makes it plain: "When a man's ways please the Lord, He makes even his enemies to be at peace with him." Supernatural favor causes God's favor to spill over into our human relationships. You don't have to work for it. You don't have to earn it. Praying in tongues unlocks it as a result of the sanctifying work of God in your life.

In Psalm 5:12 David said, "For You, O Lord, will bless the righteous; with favor You will surround him as with a shield." You are the righteousness of God in Christ Jesus, so this applies to you. Praying in tongues unleashes God's favor over our lives without any striving on our part.

Favor is "friendly regard shown toward another especially by a superior" and "approving consideration or attention" and "gracious kindness," according to *Merriam-Webster*'s dictionary. We want favor with our bosses. We want favor with our pastors. We want favor with our clients, police officers, teachers—or anyone in authority over us.

Supernatural favor causes people to consider us for promotions, raises, opportunities, and the like. Supernatural favor opens doors that no man can shut. Supernatural favor causes people to show us grace and kindness even when we don't necessarily deserve it.

David understood the favor of God like few others. He wrote, "For the Lord God is a sun and shield; the Lord bestows favor and honor. No good thing does he withhold from those who walk uprightly" (Ps. 84:11 ESV). Praying in tongues can release favor that you can't attain any other way.

Now consider this: There are two sides to grace—power and favor. One of the Greek words for *grace* is *charis*, which denotes goodwill, loving-kindness, favor, recompense, and reward, according to *The NASB New Testament Greek Lexicon*. So there's more to favor than you may have realized. Praying in tongues helps you tap into it.

King Solomon told us, "If your heart is right, favor flows from the Lord, but a devious heart invites his condemnation" (Prov. 12:2 TPT). Praying in tongues helps you keep your heart right so that flavor can flow from the throne room.

In Acts 2, right after they got filled with the Spirit they experienced great grace and favor: "So continuing daily with one accord in the temple, and breaking bread from house to house, they ate their food with gladness and simplicity of heart, praising God and having favor with all the people. And the Lord added to the church daily those who were being saved" (Acts 2:46-47).

Prayer

Father, in the name of Jesus, thank You for Your favor. As I pray in tongues, would You release Your supernatural favor over my life so even unbelievers are willing to hear what I have to say? Please, release Your favor over my life.

Empowered to Serve

You have a call of God on your life. God has given you an assignment to serve in His Kingdom. You may not be a fivefold minister, but you have a ministry.

We are all called to intercede, for example. Paul told Timothy, "Therefore I exhort first of all that supplications, prayers, intercessions, and giving of thanks be made for all men, for kings and all who are in authority, that we may lead a quiet and peaceable life in all godliness and reverence" (1 Tim. 2:1-2). We also have the ministry of reconciliation. We're called to share the good news of the gospel.

You are gifted to serve. Peter put it this way, "As each one has received a gift, minister it to one another, as good stewards of the manifold grace of God" (1 Pet. 4:10). Again, you are gifted to serve, but you are also empowered to serve. Praying in tongues empowers you to serve. The anointing God puts on your life is to serve others. The grace is to empower you to serve others.

The Amplified Classic version translates First Peter 4:10 this way: "As each of you has received a gift (a particular spiritual talent, a gracious divine endowment), employ it for one another as [befits] good trustees of God's many-sided grace [faithful stewards of the extremely diverse powers and gifts granted to Christians by unmerited favor]."

God has given you gifts; He expects you to use them in His service. It can be hard on the physical body to serve in ministry, but the Holy Spirit empowers you in your spirit, soul, and body to do what He has called you to do. Praying in tongues empowers you for the works God has called you to walk in, whether that's raising a family, working in the marketplace, serving in the government, or walking in full-time ministry.

The Message says, "Be generous with the different things God gave you, passing them around so all get in on it: if words, let it be God's words; if help, let it be God's hearty help. That way, God's bright presence will be evident in everything through Jesus, and he'll get all the credit as the One mighty in everything—encores to the end of time. Oh, yes!"

Apart from Christ we can do nothing (see John 15:15). But we are not apart from Christ. We are in Him and His Spirt is in us, empowering us to serve Him effectively for His glory. When we pray in tongues, we tap into His power to walk in the gift despite the opposition we face.

The Passion Translation offers: "Every believer has received grace gifts, so use them to serve one another as faithful stewards of the many-colored tapestry of God's grace." Pray in tongues and ask Him to empower you to walk in your gifts.

Prayer

Father, in the name of Jesus, as I pray in tongues, would You empower my spirit, soul, and body to do the work of the ministry You've called me to do? Would You help me run my race?

BENEFIT 27

Sanctifying Your Soul

The Holy Spirit is the spirit of Holy. *Holiness* means to be "set apart." Another meaning of holiness is perfection. Peter quoted from the Old Testament Book of Leviticus when he wrote, "But as He who called you is holy, you also be holy in all your conduct, because it is written, 'Be holy, for I am holy'" (1 Pet. 1:15-16).

Of course, the only perfect Man to walk the earth was Jesus, who was fully God and fully man. But the Holy Spirit is working to perfect us through sanctification. Paul prayed in First Thessalonians 5:23, "Now may the God of peace Himself sanctify you completely; and may your whole spirit, soul, and body be preserved blameless at the coming of our Lord Jesus Christ." Praying in tongues is one means to the sanctification of the Spirit.

Sanctification is the Holy Spirit's work to make us holy. We grow in holiness as we consecrate ourselves. Consecration is pulling away from something in order to draw near to something. We are pulling away from carnal endeavors to draw close to God. As we draw near to Him, He draws near to us (see James 4:8).

We know sanctification is God's will for us because Jesus asked the Father to sanctify His disciples (see John 17:17). We also see this plainly expressed in First Thessalonians 4:3, "For this is the will of God, your sanctification." *Baker's Evangelical Dictionary of Bible Theology* says:

> The generic meaning of sanctification is "the state of proper functioning." To sanctify someone or something is

to set that person or thing apart for the use intended by its designer.

A pen is "sanctified" when used to write. Eyeglasses are "sanctified" when used to improve sight. In the theological sense, things are sanctified when they are used for the purpose God intends. A human being is sanctified, therefore, when he or she lives according to God's design and purpose.

Leviticus 11:44-45, a scripture Peter quotes in his first epistle, reveals God's expectation of us: "For I am the Lord your God. You shall therefore consecrate yourselves, and you shall be holy; for I am holy. Neither shall you defile yourselves with any creeping thing that creeps on the earth. For I am the Lord who brings you up out of the land of Egypt, to be your God. You shall therefore be holy, for I am holy."

Think about it for a minute. We can't sanctify ourselves, but we can yield to the Holy Spirit's sanctification process and one way we do that and accelerate that is by praying in tongues. It's part of the mortification process I shared with you earlier.

Prayer

Father, in the name of Jesus, sanctify me. As I yield my tongue to the Spirit of Holy and allow Him to pray through me, let His work of sanctification inspire me to pull away from things that hinder love.

Working Out
Our Salvation

We were saved. We are being saved. We will be saved. This is a process known as working out our salvation, or, as some translations put it "working hard to show the results of your salvation." There should be evidence of our salvation. People should know we are different from the world. But it takes work.

Paul shared these words with the church at Philippi: "Therefore, my beloved, as you have always obeyed, not as in my presence only, but now much more in my absence, work out your own salvation with fear and trembling; for it is God who works in you both to will and to do for His good pleasure" (Phil. 2:12-13).

Praying in tongues is one way the Holy Spirit helps us work out our salvation with the fear of the Lord. As we pray in tongues, we are yielding to God's work in us to walk in His will as a citizen of the Kingdom of heaven.

We were saved when we accepted Jesus Christ as our Savior—but we can lose our salvation. Paul prophesied a Great Falling Away in Second Thessalonians 2:1-3. Paul spoke to the Corinthians about those who are "being saved" in Second Corinthians 2:15. We can also neglect our salvation, according to Hebrews 2:1-2. Peter tells us to be careful to make our calling and election sure in Second Peter 1:10.

Finally, we will be saved. This is salvation in the future tense, in these sense of the Second Coming of Jesus Christ. In Matthew 25:46, Jesus speaks of the righteous entering eternal life. In Romans 5:9-10 Paul writes to the church at Roman and speaks of a time when "we shall be saved."

In Romans 13:11, Paul tells the church their salvation is nearer now than when they first believed (or when they were first saved). And First Thessalonians 5:8 speaks of the hope of our salvation.

Why do we have to hope for something we have? Because we're hoping for the culmination of that salvation when there will be no more weeping, no more pain, no more devil forever and ever. Praying in tongues helps us work out our salvation. It's not about a work of the flesh. Rather, it's cooperating with Jesus to complete the good work He started in you, according to Philippians 2:12, which reads:

> *Therefore, my dear ones, as you have always obeyed [my suggestions], so now, not only [with the enthusiasm you would show] in my presence but much more because I am absent, work out (cultivate, carry out to the goal, and fully complete) your own salvation with reverence and awe and trembling (self-distrust, with serious caution, tenderness of conscience, watchfulness against temptation, timidly shrinking from whatever might offend God and discredit the name of Christ)* (AMPC).

Prayer

Father, in the name of Jesus, I want to see the culmination of Your glorious salvation in my life. As I pray in tongues, strengthen me to keep walking as a child of God, confident that whatever I walk through will be worth it at the end of the age.

BENEFIT 29

Hear God's Voice More Clearly

We all have the ability to hear the voice of the Lord. Remember when Jesus said, "My sheep hear My voice, and I know them, and they follow Me" (John 10:27)? The Holy Spirit transmits the voice of Jesus to your spirit. The Holy Spirit gives you the testimony—what Jesus is saying—of Jesus.

The challenge is there are many voices in the spirit competing for our attention—and sometimes they are louder than the voice of God in our life. Praying in tongues gives you a stronger antenna to pick up that voice clearly, hearing through the demonic static and even the thoughts of your own mind.

When I first started traveling in itinerant ministry, my ministry partner was always praying in tongues during the worship, then prophesying. He would prophesy and ask me, "You got something?" Often, I didn't. I was discerning spirits in the room. I had to train myself, like he did, to pray in tongues and listen for what God wanted to say. You can do the same.

One reason why praying in tongues helps you hear the voice of God more clearly is because we are being intentional. We are sowing to the Spirit. And we're not as distracted by natural things. Jesus said, "However, when He, the Spirit of truth, has come, He will guide you into all truth; for He will not speak on His own authority, but whatever He hears He will speak; and He will tell you things to come. He will glorify Me, for He will take of what is Mine and declare it to you" (John 16:13-14).

Think about it and consider how much sense this makes. When we pray in tongues, we're giving ourselves over to the Holy Spirit's direction. We're becoming more sensitive to His still small voice in our spirits. The Holy Spirit is your personal prophet and you can tap into His prophetic utterance for you—and for other people—by praying in tongues.

The New Living Translation puts it this way: "When the Spirit of truth comes, he will guide you into all truth. He will not speak on his own but will tell you what he has heard. He will tell you about the future. He will bring me glory by telling you whatever he receives from me." Praying in tongues helps you tap into that voice of truth.

Finally, *The Passion Translation* really drives it home: "But when the truth-giving Spirit comes, he will unveil the reality of every truth within you. He won't speak on his own, but only what he hears from the Father, and he will reveal prophetically to you what is to come. He will glorify me on the earth, for he will receive from me what is mine and reveal it to you."

If you want to hear the voice of Jesus more clearly, praying in tongues will open your spirit and your mind to hear the Holy Spirit's transmission of what the Head of the church wants to tell you.

Prayer

Father, in the name of Jesus, I want to hear the voice of Jesus with crystal clarity. As I pray in tongues, help me discern better Your voice from among the many voices in the spirit realm—and even my own thoughts.

Equipped to Minister Life

We all have a ministry. You may not have a public speaking ministry or a deliverance ministry or a prophetic ministry, but you have a ministry of reconciliation, according to Second Corinthians 5:18. You have a ministry.

Paul wrote, "Who also made us sufficient as ministers of the new covenant, not of the letter but of the Spirit; for the letter kills, but the Spirit gives life" (2 Cor. 3:6). We're no longer under the Law but under grace. As such, we need to minister life to believers and pre-believers alike. Jesus ministered life; so should we. As a matter of fact, He clearly said He didn't come into the world to condemn people but to offer them salvation (see John 3:17).

Angry preachers mispresent Jesus. Religious preachers misrepresent Jesus. Praying in tongues equips us to minister life by giving us a revelation of who God is, not who religion has painted Him to be. Praying in tongues uproots the anger and judgment we've experienced in our own church experiences and therefore model to the world.

The Amplified Classic translation Second Corinthians 5:18 reveals: "[It is He] Who has qualified us [making us to be fit and worthy and sufficient] as ministers and dispensers of a new covenant [of salvation through Christ], not [ministers] of the letter (of legally written code) but of the Spirit; for the code [of the Law] kills, but the [Holy] Spirit makes alive."

Have you ever heard preachers who minister condemnation, doom, and gloom? Their messages have a sharp edge that is critical and shaming.

That's not the Holy Spirit. Those preachers need a good dose of the Holy Ghost! Praying in tongues helps you minister the life of God to God's New Covenant people. I'm not saying people don't need challenging messages or to be corrected, but love brings us into life, not death.

The Message translation of Second Corinthians 3:6 tells us, "Only God can write such a letter. His letter authorizes us to help carry out this new plan of action. The plan wasn't written out with ink on paper, with pages and pages of legal footnotes, killing your spirit. It's written with Spirit on spirit, his life on our lives!"

Have you ever heard prophets who only prophesy judgment? They need a fresh infilling of the Holy Spirit and a deep encounter with the good, good Father. Although God is the Judge, He's also the Bridegroom and King. We are in a new dispensation, a dispensation of grace. God is still Judge, but He's not dooming His people to misery. Praying in tongues roots out of us self-judgment and self-condemnation that causes us to represent God incorrectly as we minister.

Our flesh can rise up. Our unrenewed mind can be critical. We want to minister life. We want to counsel people with hope. We want to inspire faith and, when necessary, repentance. It is the kindness of God that leads people to repentance, not judgment and criticism (see Rom. 2:4). Any of us can tap into this, but praying in tongues helps us to minister life.

Prayer

Father, in the name of Jesus, I want to minister life, not death. As I pray in tongues, give me a heart of compassion for people, saved and pre-saved, and help me minister with Christ's heart to help people live in victory.

BENEFIT 31

Tapping into God's Peace

I once asked a friend if she could pick between peace and joy, which would she pick? She said peace. If you have peace, she said, likely you'll have joy. Thank God, we don't have to choose. We can have it all as Kingdom citizens. Paul the apostle said, "For the kingdom of God is not eating and drinking, but righteousness and peace and joy in the Holy Spirit" (Rom. 14:17).

Think about it. The Holy Spirit is the Spirit of peace. When you pray in tongues, you are tapping into the very Spirit of peace. When you feel anxious you can cast your cares on the Lord and pray in tongues and peace will come. As one who struggled with anxiety for years, I can tell you it brings near-immediate relief.

Isaiah tapped into a truth in the face of the persecution he experienced as a prophet. His revelation centuries ago is our revelation today: "You will keep him in perfect peace, whose mind is stayed on You, because he trusts in You" (Isa. 26:3).

When you lose your peace, praying in tongues demonstrates an effort to put your mind on God and trust Him. Paul wrote, "And let the peace of God rule in your hearts, to which also you were called in one body; and be thankful" (Col. 3:15). When we pray in tongues, we are choosing peace. We could be speaking words of worry, but instead we are speaking words that edify us.

Peace can be hard to come by in a chaotic world. The enemy sets you up to get you upset and steal your peace. But Jesus left His peace with us, and the Spirit of Peace has made His home in us. We must learn to appropriate the peace of God. We can do that by thanking Him for His peace, but we can also do that by praying in tongues.

Paul wrote, "For to be carnally minded is death, but to be spiritually minded is life and peace" (Rom. 8:6). When you are praying in tongues, you are being spiritually minded and it leads to peace where stress and worry are trying to overcome you. And Paul assured us in Philippians 4:6-7, "Be anxious for nothing, but in everything by prayer and supplication, with thanksgiving, let your requests be made known to God; and the peace of God, which surpasses all understanding, will guard your hearts and minds through Christ Jesus."

Sometimes we cast our cares and take them back, or we try to cast our cares but just can't seem to cast them far enough away from our soul to stop thinking about them. Praying in tongues helps us tap into the peace of God that passes all understanding that guards our hearts and minds through Christ Jesus.

Prayer

Father, in the name of Jesus, I want to walk in the peace that passes all understanding. As I pray in tongues, would You help me tap into that supernatural peace? Would You inspire me to pray in tongues when the enemy comes to steal my peace?

Experiencing God's Joy

We know peace is our portion, but so is joy. Thankfully, we don't have to pick and choose. We can have it all in abundance. Paul wrote, "For the kingdom of God is not eating and drinking, but righteousness and peace and joy in the Holy Spirit" (Rom. 14:17).

Just as praying in tongues can help you tap into the peace of God, praying in tongues can help you tap into the joy of the Lord, which is your strength. Nehemiah brought us this revelation in Nehemiah 8:10 (NLT): "Don't be dejected and sad, for the joy of the Lord is your strength!" You can tap into this joy by praying in tongues.

The enemy is what we might call a killjoy. He comes after your car or your promotion or your money. At the end of the day, he's not really after your car or your promotion or your money. He has no real use of these things. Rather, he wants to steal your joy because he knows this joy is the source of strength you need to resist him.

Without joy, it's hard to have hope, and without hope you can't have faith because faith is the substance of things hoped for (see Heb. 11:1). We're not talking about happiness here, but joy. Happiness may be circumstantial, but the joy of the Lord holds steady in every circumstance. Indeed, the joy of the Lord is based on only one circumstance—your salvation (see Ps. 51:12).

The joy of the Lord is the joy the Lord Himself gives us. It's part of His private stash of joy, which is inexhaustible. We can be happy in life when things go our way, but the joy that comes from the Lord will sustain us when everything that can go wrong is going wrong. One way we release that joy into our lives is through praying in tongues.

Another word for *joy* is *gladness*. Bible lexicons often use joy and gladness interchangeably. *Merriam-Webster*'s dictionary defines *gladness* as "experiencing pleasure, joy, or delight." God wants us to take pleasure in Him and delight in Him. Praying in tongues is one way to get in that river of joy.

Merriam-Webster's dictionary also defines *gladness* as "marked by, expressive of, or caused by happiness and joy." The devil wants to mark us with defeat, discouragement, and death. But the Lord wants to mark us with joy—the gladness the Bible speaks about. We position ourselves to receive and feel the joy of the Lord when we pray in tongues.

David said, "You have put gladness in my heart, more than in the season that their grain and wine increased" (Ps. 4:7). We're not talking about a fleeting moment of glee here. *The Passion Translation* of Psalm 4:7 puts it this way, "The intense pleasure you give me surpasses the gladness of harvest time." This is joyful release, rejoicing with joy inexpressible and full of glory (1 Pet. 1:8).

Remember, in His presence is fullness of joy (see Ps. 16:11). Praying in tongues with a mind to tap into His joy can unlock an experience you won't soon forget.

Prayer

Father, in the name of Jesus, would You help me to live in a constant state of joy, regardless of my circumstances, as I pray in tongues? Would You help me to feel Your very own river of joy that never runs dry?

Sensitive to the Holy Spirit's Emotions

The Holy Spirit is a Person. He is more real than you or me. He is the Third Person of the Godhead. The Holy Spirit is just as much God as the Father and Jesus are God. It's a great mystery we call the Trinity—and God has emotions.

Maybe you've never considered that the Holy Spirit has emotions, which are diverse. Of course, His emotions are not wishy-washy like ours can be at times. His emotions are not unstable. His emotions don't depend on what the flesh dictates.

When we pray in tongues, we are more sensitive to the Holy Spirit's emotions. Of course, His emotions are holy. His emotions are appropriate for every situation. Our emotions are sometimes influenced by past hurts or traumas—or even demons. One way we can discern His leadership is by experiencing His emotions in any given situation.

We know the Holy Spirit can be grieved. Ephesians 4:30 tells us, "And do not grieve the Holy Spirit of God, by whom you were sealed for the day of redemption." And again, "But they rebelled and grieved His Holy Spirit; so He turned Himself against them as an enemy, and He fought against them" (Isa. 63:10).

Many Christians seem to have no idea that they are grieving the Holy Spirit with their words, thoughts, and behaviors because they are not in tune with His emotions. Like David, we need to be a student of God's emotions. We need to understand how He feels about people, places, and things so we can respond according to His will.

Likewise, the Holy Spirit can be insulted. Hebrews 10:29 reads, "Of how much worse punishment, do you suppose, will he be thought worthy who has trampled the Son of God underfoot, counted the blood of the covenant by which he was sanctified a common thing, and insulted the Spirit of grace?"

The Holy Spirit can be vexed, which means irritated, annoyed, or frustrated. Psalm 78:41 reveals, "Again and again they put God to the test; they vexed the Holy One of Israel" (NIV). Of course, He's not insulted or vexed the same way we are. He doesn't act outside love despite these emotions. His emotions are not defiled by sin.

The Holy Spirit loves (see 1 John 4:8). The Holy Spirit hates (see Prov. 6:16). The Holy Spirit gets jealous (see Exod. 20:5). The Holy Spirit feels joy (see Zeph. 3:17). The Holy Spirit laughs (see Ps. 2:4). The Holy Spirit feels compassion (see Ps. 135:14).

Praying in tongues helps us align with the Holy Spirit's emotions. When we align with His emotions, we can respond more properly to challenges and circumstances. Instead of manifesting emotional instability, we can understand how the Holy Spirit feels and lean into His grace to walk through emotional situations.

Prayer

Father, in the name of Jesus, spur me to be a student of Your emotions so I can understand how You really feel about me and others. As I pray in tongues, would You help me tune into Your holy emotions and stabilize my own erratic emotions?

Intercede More Effectively

Although I do believe there is a gift of intercession that manifests in the lives of some Christians, we're all called to make intercession. Yes, every one of us is called to petition God on behalf of others. Prayer is talking to God. Intercession is talking to God on behalf of others—pleading someone else's case to God. Praying in tongues helps you make more effective intercession.

Paul made this plain in First Timothy 2:1, "Therefore I exhort first of all that supplications, prayers, intercessions, and giving of thanks be made for all men." And again, at the end of Paul's exhortation on the hierarchy of demons and the whole armor of God, Paul said this: "Praying always with all prayer and supplication in the Spirit, being watchful to this end with all perseverance and supplication for all the saints" (Eph. 6:18).

When we are standing in the role of intercessor, we are exercising a ministry that our Lord Jesus Christ is also actively demonstrating in heaven. Romans 8:34 tells us, "Who is he who condemns? It is Christ who died, and furthermore is also risen, who is even at the right hand of God, who also makes intercession for us." And Hebrews 7:25 confirms, "Therefore He is also able to save to the uttermost those who come to God through Him, since He always lives to make intercession for them."

When we make intercession, we're acting like Christ. It's selfless. The difference is Christ knows exactly how to intercede for anyone or anything. He always releases a perfect prayer. But we don't always know how to make intercession for something or someone. We don't always know how to pray. Praying in tongues helps us intercede more strategically.

Romans 8:26 explains, "Likewise, the Spirit helps us in our weaknesses, for we do not know what to pray for as we ought, but the Spirit Himself intercedes for us with groanings too deep for words" (MEV). When we pray in tongues, we're praying a perfect prayer for someone according to God's will.

We can lift up someone's name and tell God we don't know how to pray for them with our natural understanding, then ask the Holy Spirit to help us pray for them as we give voice to His utterance by releasing our heavenly prayer language. The Holy Spirit can plead for them through us as we pray in tongues.

Indeed, part of the mystery of praying in tongues is we may never know what we prayed. We might not be daring enough to pray in English what we prayed in the Spirit. If we knew what we were praying, we may not think it's the most effective prayer strategy—but the Holy Spirit's prayer strategy is always the best intercession strategy. When we pray in tongues, our mind is unfruitful but our intercession is perfect.

Prayer

Father, in the name of Jesus, I acknowledge that I don't always have the right intercessory prayer strategy. As I pray in tongues with a mind toward intercession for a person or place, help me see the fruit of these prayers so I can glorify You all the more.

Activate Seer Eyes

Just as I believe God is speaking more than we're hearing (or listening), I believe the Holy Spirit is trying to show us things to come—or show us what the Father is doing—more than we're seeing. Praying in tongues can activate our seer eyes to see what He wants us to see in the spirit.

Just like all believers can prophesy according to the will of God, all believers can see in the spirit when God chooses to open their eyes. Seeing is part of the gift of prophecy—it's just another dimension of the prophetic gift mix. Paul offers revelation on the gifts of the Spirit in First Corinthians 12:7-11:

> But the manifestation of the Spirit is given to everyone for the common good. To one is given by the Spirit the word of wisdom, to another the word of knowledge by the same Spirit, to another faith by the same Spirit, to another gifts of healings by the same Spirit, to another the working of miracles, to another prophecy, to another discerning of spirits, to another various kinds of tongues, and to another the interpretation of tongues. But that one and very same Spirit works all these, dividing to each one individually as He will (MEV).

Any believer can manifest any of the gifts of the Spirit any time God sees fit. His gifts are to bless people, whether saved or lost. We cannot choose to work a miracle, but we can believe in faith to walk in the miracle realm. We cannot choose to interpret tongues, but we can yield to the Holy Spirit if He chooses to give us an interpretation.

Much the same, we cannot force the spirit realm open and take a peek, but we can ask the Lord to open our eyes to show us what He wants us to see and walk with a sensitivity that makes us more aware of what He wants to show us. Praying in tongues opens the eyes of our heart—our spiritual eyes—in conjunction with Paul's prayer in Ephesians 1:18:

> *I pray that the eyes of your heart may be enlightened in order that you may know the hope to which he has called you, the riches of his glorious inheritance in his holy people* (NIV).

The Amplified Bible puts it this way:

> *And [I pray] that the eyes of your heart [the very center and core of your being] may be enlightened [flooded with light by the Holy Spirit], so that you will know and cherish the hope [the divine guarantee, the confident expectation] to which He has called you, the riches of His glorious inheritance in the saints (God's people).*

Praying in tongues invites the Holy Spirit to flood your spiritual eyes with the light—opening them to seer dimensions you haven't experienced before. Ask the Holy Spirit to open and activate your seer eyes, then pray in tongues consistently with this in mind and watch what happens!

Prayer

Father, in the name of Jesus, I want to see what You are trying to show me. As I pray in tongues, will You open my seer eyes? Will You flood my eyes with Your glorious light so I can receive visual intelligence from Your Spirit?

Tame Your Tongue

If we're honest, we will admit we have a problem with our mouths. That wagging tongue gets us in trouble. At times, our speech is not edifying to others or ourselves. Or, more accurately, sometimes we speak the power of death instead of the power of life. We word-curse others and ourselves with our anointed mouths. Praying in tongues can help us overcome the dangers of our untamed mouth.

Peter was clear: "For he who would love life and see good days, let him refrain his tongue from evil, and his lips from speaking deceit" (1 Pet. 3:10). And Paul offered this Spirit-inspired command: "Let no corrupt word proceed out of your mouth, but what is good for necessary edification, that it may impart grace to the hearers" (Eph. 4:29).

We can't consistently obey these words without Holy Spirit's help. But thank God when we pray in tongues we won't say anything wrong. What's more, when we pray in tongues we are positioning ourselves to allow the Holy Spirit to tame our tongues. James, the apostle of practical faith, made it clear:

> But no man can tame the tongue. It is an unruly evil, full of deadly poison. With it we bless our God and Father, and with it we curse men, who have been made in the similitude of God. Out of the same mouth proceed blessing and cursing. My brethren, these things ought not to be so. Does a spring send forth fresh water and bitter from the same opening? Can a fig tree, my brethren, bear olives, or a grapevine bear figs? Thus no spring yields both salt water and fresh (James 3:8-12).

Believe me, you need to tame your tongue! And I need to tame mine. But, again, you can't and I can't do it by force of our will alone. We need the Holy Spirit's help. And it's critical that we lean into this because Proverbs 10:19 assures, "In the multitude of words sin is not lacking, but he who restrains his lips is wise."

Proverbs 21:23 makes it clear: "Whoever guards his mouth and tongue keeps his soul from troubles." And Jesus Himself said, "Not what goes into the mouth defiles a man; but what comes out of the mouth, this defiles a man" (Matt. 15:11). In case you aren't convinced, consider *The Message* version of James 3:7-10:

> *This is scary: You can tame a tiger, but you can't tame a tongue—it's never been done. The tongue runs wild, a wanton killer. With our tongues we bless God our Father; with the same tongues we curse the very men and women he made in his image. Curses and blessings out of the same mouth!*

Scary indeed! We can hurt people with our mouths. We can stumble into sin through gossip. We can come into agreement with the enemy's plans through complaining. When you are tempted to say something out of order, begin praying in tongues instead. That will stop death from coming out of your mouth and will help you tame your tongue.

Prayer

Father, in the name of Jesus, I repent for my unruly tongue. Remind me to pray in tongues when I am tempted to speak out of line. When I pray in tongues, yielding my tongue to Your Spirit, would You tame my tongue so I can grow in gracious speech?

Strength in Tribulation

We all have tribulations in life. You can't pray them away—but you can pray your way through. Those aren't my words. They are the words of Jesus Himself. Jesus said, "These things I have spoken to you, that in Me you may have peace. In the world you will have tribulation; but be of good cheer, I have overcome the world" (John 16:33).

One of the best ways to tap into God's strength in the midst of tribulation is praying in tongues. Indeed, praying in tongues helps us walk through our trials with our heads held high. Praying in tongues gives us endurance in tribulation, which is unavoidable.

The Amplified Bible, Classic Edition emphasizes this truth: "In the world you have tribulation and trials and distress and frustration; but be of good cheer [take courage; be confident, certain, undaunted]! For I have overcome the world. [I have deprived it of power to harm you and have conquered it for you.]"

Notice how the Amplified breaks it down. Not every tribulation is earth-shattering, some of them are just distress or—how about this—frustration. Praying in tongues in the midst of this process helps us to take courage and be confident, certain, and undaunted.

I like that word *undaunted*. It means, "courageously resolute especially in the face of danger or difficulty: not discouraged," according to *Merriam-Webster*'s dictionary. Let's face it. When trials come sometimes we're daunted. Sometimes the enemy's fire subdues our fire. But we can pray in tongues and be of good cheer.

Think about it for a minute. When tribulation comes, it usually takes us by surprise. It's an unwelcome suddenly and it takes us off guard. When the tribulation hits, we usually have no idea how to pray and may not even feel like praying. Praying in tongues helps us to be of good cheer in the trial.

The Good News Translation puts it this way: "The world will make you suffer. But be brave! I have defeated the world!" *The Message* says, "In this godless world you will continue to experience difficulties. But take heart! I've conquered the world." And *The Passion Translation* tells us, "For in this unbelieving world you will experience trouble and sorrows, but you must be courageous, for I have conquered the world!"

Pray in tongues through your trouble and sorrows! You'll make your way through with more courage. We don't want to get in the middle of the tribulation and camp out there. We don't want to stay there longer than we have to. Praying in tongues will lead you through to the other side, where breakthrough awaits.

The key is remembering to do that, right? Sometimes in the midst of trouble we forget to do what we know to do. That's why making a habit of praying in tongues is so vital to your successful Christian living. When something is a habit, you don't have to think about it! It just kicks in!

Prayer

Father, in the name of Jesus, thank You for warning me that I will face tribulation. And thank You, even more, for helping me walk through tribulation with good cheer as I pray in tongues. Help me to walk through tribulation with peace.

BENEFIT 38

Discover Your Purpose

D o you know your purpose? Do you have a revelation on what God created you to do? God has a purpose for your life. He's not wondering what your purpose is. He knows—and He wants you to know. Praying in tongues is one way the Holy Spirit helps us discover our purpose.

If you don't know your purpose, you are not alone. Indeed, most Christians aren't sure of their purpose or calling or when they get a fleeting glimpse they don't know how to walk in their prophetic destiny.

Here's the good news: God is not trying to hide our purpose from us. Paul explained, "For we are His workmanship, created in Christ Jesus for good works, which God prepared beforehand that we should walk in them" (Eph. 2:10).

How can we walk in good works if we don't know what they are? If praying in tongues can unlock revelation and mysteries, and Scripture says it can, then praying in tongues can certainly help us discover our purpose.

The Berean Study Bible translates Ephesians 2:10 this way: "For we are God's workmanship, created in Christ Jesus to do good works, which God prepared in advance as our way of life." God prepared the good works before you were born. He knows what He purposed you to do. Praying in tongues helps us get the mind of Christ on our purpose.

The New Living Translation explains: "For we are God's masterpiece. He has created us anew in Christ Jesus, so we can do the good things he planned for us long ago." God has not forgotten your purpose. All the days of your life are written in a book. Praying in tongues helps you access the intel you need to walk in your purpose.

The Passion Translation says, "We have become his poetry, a re-created people that will fulfill the destiny he has given each of us, for we are joined to Jesus, the Anointed One. Even before we were born, God planned in advance our destiny and the good works we would do to fulfill it!" You have a prophetic destiny. Praying in tongues not only helps you discover it, but helps you walk in it. The Amplified Classic version reads:

> *For we are God's [own] handiwork (His workmanship), recreated in Christ Jesus, [born anew] that we may do those good works which God predestined (planned beforehand) for us [taking paths which He prepared ahead of time], that we should walk in them [living the good life which He prearranged and made ready for us to live].*

Catch that: "taking paths which He prepared ahead of time" and "living the good life which He prearranged and made ready for us to live." God has done His part. We have to do our part. He's made the preparations for you to walk in your purpose. Praying in tongues helps us discover what we're called to do and then do that and only that.

Prayer

Father, in the name of Jesus, thank You that Your purpose for my life is glorious. As I pray in tongues, would You help me unlock understanding of Your special purpose for me in the earth?

Courage to Deny Self

Jesus was painfully clear: "If anyone desires to come after Me, let him deny himself, and take up his cross daily, and follow Me" (Luke 9:23). This is a heavy statement. There's no way to sugarcoat this verse—and it takes great courage to consistently deny oneself. Praying in tongues gives you grace to obey this command.

In the Amplified Classic translation, Jesus' statement is even heavier: "And He said to all, If any person wills to come after Me, let him deny himself [disown himself, forget, lose sight of himself and his own interests, refuse and give up himself] and take up his cross daily and follow Me [cleave steadfastly to Me, conform wholly to My example in living and, if need be, in dying also]."

Jesus wants us to willfully follow Him, and it takes a strong will to do so because the world wants to bend your will to its ways. God's ways are higher than our ways and sometimes make no sense to the natural mind. The good news is praying in tongues will help you disown your rights, forget what you want, and lose sight of your own interests for the sake of Christ's interests.

The Passion Translation puts it this way: "Jesus said to all of his followers, 'If you truly desire to be my disciple, you must disown your life completely, embrace my "cross" as your own, and surrender to my ways.'"

Here's the deal: Self will never deny self. The flesh wars against the Spirit and the Spirit wars against the flesh (see Gal. 5:17). Praying in tongues will help you deny yourself so you can truly be a disciple of Christ.

Now, Jesus doesn't stop there with this type of talk. In Luke 14:27, "Whoever does not persevere and carry his own cross and come after (follow) Me cannot be My disciple" (AMPC). How can we possibly do that? We have to get our souls on the side of the Holy Spirit because our flesh will never agree. Praying in tongues helps us to be willing to deny ourselves and pick up the cross.

Jesus goes on to say, "So then, any of you who does not forsake (renounce, surrender claim to, give up, say good-bye to) all that he has cannot be My disciple" (Luke 14:33 AMPC). Jesus isn't letting go of this concept. He's drilling it into our heads. Apart from Christ we can't do this. But when we pray in tongues, the Holy Spirit helps us deny ourselves and carry that cross and be true disciples of Christ.

Matthew 10:38 continues the theme. Jesus said, "And he who does not take up his cross and follow Me [cleave steadfastly to Me, conforming wholly to My example in living and, if need be, in dying also] is not worthy of Me" (AMPC).

This is heavy, but all things are possible to him who believes (see Mark 9:23). We must commit to praying in tongues for many reasons, but this is one of the most serious.

Prayer

Father, in the name of Jesus, I want to follow You completely. As I pray in tongues, please give me the grace and courage to deny myself and embrace the work of the cross.

Entering into God's Rest

We all need to rest, but in this busy world, rest—both natural and spiritual—must be intentional. Many of us are running on fumes and have no time to stop and fill back up again. The good news is praying in tongues—which you can do just about anywhere—helps you enter into the rest of God.

Consider Isaiah 28:11-12, "For with stammering lips and another tongue He will speak to this people, to whom He said, 'This is the rest with which You may cause the weary to rest,' and, 'This is the refreshing.'" Again, praying in tongues helps you experience God's refreshing.

We need rest for our souls and our bodies—and we can even feel weary in the things of the spirit when we move beyond the grace of God. If you want to avoid burnout, consistently pray in tongues.

The Passion Translation translates our verse this way: "With stammering lips and in a foreign language he will speak to this people. For he has said to them, 'This is your rest, so let the weary rest; this is your comfort'—but they would not listen." Did you hear that? If so, listen.

Praying in tongues brings you into rest. It helps you focus on the reality that in Christ we can have rest, even when there's chaos and turmoil, trials, and tribulation. Praying in tongues helps you rise above the chaos and enter into the refreshing.

Hebrews 4:9-11 relates, "There remains therefore a rest for the people of God. For he who has entered His rest has himself also ceased from his works as God did from His. Let us therefore be diligent to enter that rest, lest anyone fall according to the same example of disobedience."

Whatever it is you are dealing with, there is a place of rest for you to enter into. Now, this is not resting from the work but resting in the work. When we enter God's rest, we don't have to figure everything out and run around in circles. That's a powerful concept to understand. Praying in tongues can still our soul.

Jesus said, "Come to Me, all you who labor and are heavy laden, and I will give you rest. Take My yoke upon you and learn from Me, for I am gentle and lowly in heart, and you will find rest for your souls. For My yoke is easy and My burden is light" (Matt. 11:28-30). One way you come to Jesus is through praying in tongues. It's not the only way, but it is a powerful way.

David understood this. In Psalm 23:1-3, he wrote, "The Lord is my shepherd; I shall not want. He makes me to lie down in green pastures; He leads me beside the still waters. He restores my soul." Praying in tongues brings rest, restoration, and refreshing to the soul.

Prayer

Father, in the name of Jesus, I grow weary at times and forget to come to You. Help me remember to turn toward You,, praying in tongues to enter into Your glorious rest for my soul and body.

BENEFIT 41

Worship God
in Spirit and in Truth

When Jesus met the woman at the well, He not only told her everything about her life, He shared with this Samaritan woman some deep spiritual truths. One of those truths related to how we worship the Lord our God.

Jesus told the woman, "God is Spirit, and those who worship Him must worship in spirit and truth" (John 4:24). When we pray in tongues, our spirit is praying. Just like we're releasing the perfect prayer in tongues, we're releasing the perfect worship in tongues. Think about that for a minute!

The Passion Translation puts it this way: "For God is a Spirit, and he longs to have sincere worshipers who adore him in the realm of the Spirit and in truth." Have you ever started singing in tongues during worship? This is the Holy Spirit helping you worship Jesus.

The Message tells us, "God is sheer being itself—Spirit. Those who worship him must do it out of their very being, their spirits, their true selves, in adoration."

When we worship in tongues, we're not merely going through the motions. We're not just singing a song and clapping our hands. We're worshiping with a sincere heart. Our spirit is worshiping the Spirit of God. When can go to another level of worship when we sing in the spirit.

Remember, you are a spirit, you have a soul, and you live in a body. When we sing in the spirit, we worship out of our very being, our spirits, our true selves, in adoration. It's not soulish excitement, though there's nothing wrong with that. Jesus said we should love the Lord our God with all of our mind, all of our heart, all of our soul, and all of our strength (see Luke 10:27).

Take a look at this reality in Acts 10:44-46, "While Peter was still speaking these words, the Holy Spirit fell upon all those who heard the word. And those of the circumcision who believed were astonished, as many as came with Peter, because the gift of the Holy Spirit had been poured out on the Gentiles also. For they heard them speak with tongues and magnify God."

When we sing in tongues, we are magnifying God. Remember, there is no brain activity in the frontal lobe when we pray in the spirit. This is pure worship in spirit and in truth. If we don't know how to pray as we ought, it's not a stretch to say we don't know how to worship as we ought. We can go deeper in worship, at times, in tongues.

When we sing in tongues, we're worshiping in the splendor of holiness (see Ps. 29:2). We are worshiping at His footstool (see Ps. 99:5). We are singing praises to His name (see Ps. 66:4). We are singing spiritual songs (see Col. 3:16).

Prayer

Father, in the name of Jesus, help me sing the song of the Lord. Help me worship You in spirit and in truth, singing spiritual songs in worship to Your holy name.

Receiving Holy Boldness

If we are going to walk in consistent victory, we need to walk in consistent boldness. The enemy of your soul is bold in his efforts to steal, kill, and destroy (see John 10:10). People are bold in their demands on your life. Sometimes you have to release a bold prayer. Other times you need to release a bold "no!"

What is boldness? *Bold* means "fearless before danger," and "showing or requiring a fearless, daring spirit," according to *Merriam-Webster*'s dictionary. The disciples in the early church had to be bold in preaching the gospel—fearless about the potential consequences. The persecution was real.

When Peter and John were arrested, threatened, and released for healing the man at the Gate Beautiful, they went back to their own company and reported what happened. Then they prayed for boldness. Acts 4:31 offers the results of that prayer meeting: "the place where they were assembled together was shaken; and they were all filled with the Holy Spirit, and they spoke the word of God with boldness."

The Greek word for *boldness* in that verse is *parrhesia*. According to *The KJV Greek New Testament Greek Lexicon*, it means "freedom in speaking, unreservedness in speech, free and fearless confidence, cheerful courage, boldness, assurance."

That's how we want to think, talk, and walk as a Christian. I don't want to be timid. I don't want to run from the battle line. I don't want to avoid difficult conversations. I want a holy boldness! When we pray in tongues we get bolder over time.

The Amplified Classic version translates Acts 4:31 tells us, "And when they had prayed, the place in which they were assembled was shaken; and they were all filled with the Holy Spirit, and they continued to speak the Word of God with freedom and boldness and courage."

When you are filled with the Spirit, boldness will come upon you. If you are not feeling particularly bold, pray in tongues until you do. Maybe you are nervous about speaking in public—pray in tongues for boldness. Proverbs 28:1 tells us, "The righteous are bold as a lion." You are the righteousness of God in Christ Jesus, according to Second Corinthians 5:21.

In Christ, you "have boldness and access with confidence through faith in Him" (Eph. 3:12). You have boldness on the inside of you because the Christ in you is bold. Praying in tongues will help you tap into that boldness when you are feeling timid or intimidated.

God wants us to be bold in the face of enemy opposition. In fact, He commanded Joshua more than once to be bold. Joshua 1:9 tells us, "Have I not commanded you? Be strong and of good courage; do not be afraid, nor be dismayed, for the Lord your God is with you wherever you go."

Joshua didn't have the capability of praying in tongues because the Holy Spirit was not yet poured out. We do. Let's take advantage of this gift of tongues to increase our boldness.

Prayer

Father, in the name of Jesus, would You inspire me to pray in tongues when intimidating circumstances are trying to overtake me? Deliver me from timidity and make me brave and bold.

Receiving Physical Healing

C an you really receive physical healing through praying in tongues? Yes. Your body is the temple of the Holy Spirit, according to First Corinthians 16:9. The Holy Spirit is interested in living in a healthy house rather than a broken-down, beat-up house.

Think about it for a minute. If you could choose to live in a newly refurbished house or a moldy house with termites, which would you choose? There's no question. And remember, it's always God's will to heal, even if you have abused your body and made poor health choices. You can repent and receive healing.

Praying in tongues can manifest healing to your physical body. That probably doesn't make any sense to your mind, but it makes perfect sense in God's mind. The Holy Spirit is the power that heals. Therefore, when we yield our tongue to His utterance for healing needs, we position ourselves to receive healing.

Consider this: Jude 20 tell us, "But you, beloved, building yourselves up on your most holy faith, praying in the Holy Spirit." Now, the Greek word for *building* in that verse is *epoikodomeo*, which means "to build up," according to *The NASB New Testament Greek Lexicon*.

What's more, First Corinthians 14:4 tells us, "He who speaks in a tongue edifies himself." That Greek word for *edifies* in that verse is *oikodomeo*. According to *The KJV New Testament Greek Lexicon*, *edify* in this verse means, "to build a house, erect a building" and "to restore by building, to rebuild, repair."

Who are you? You are a spirit who lives in your body. So is the Holy Spirit. He is a spirit who lives in your body. He has made your spirit His home. So when you pray in tongues, the Holy Spirit is not just building you up, He's rebuilding and repairing His temple. You could say, "He who prays in tongues restores, rebuilds, and repairs himself."

Your spirit is not damaged, so your spirit doesn't need repairing. Our outward man is perishing, but our inward man is renewed day by day (see 2 Cor. 4:16). Moses was old and his eyes did not grow dim (see Deut. 24:7). He did not die of a heart attack or cancer. He just went home to the Lord.

When you pray in tongues with a mind toward healing, I believe the Holy Spirit also joins with your prayer because He wants you healed and whole. First Peter 2:24 expresses it is God's will to heal: "who Himself bore our sins in His own body on the tree, that we, having died to sins, might live for righteousness—by whose stripes you were healed." If you were healed, then you are healed. You just have to tap into that healing power.

Psalm 103:2-4 reads, "Bless the Lord, O my soul, and forget not all His benefits: who forgives all your iniquities, who heals all your diseases, who redeems your life from destruction." When you pray in tongues, you are tapping into these benefits and into healing power when your body needs it. Keep praying in tongues no matter how long it takes.

Prayer

Father, in the name of Jesus, You are my Healer—and Your healing power dwells on the inside of me. As I pray in tongues, would You heal me completely? Whether little by little or suddenly at once, Father, heal me.

BENEFIT 44

Find Inner Healing

If God can heal your physical body, don't you think He can bring inner healing? Don't you think He can heal your soul, your emotions? Yes, He can. You may need inner healing because someone wounded you, but the reason you stay hurt is not because you got hurt.

Let me put it this way. If break your leg, it heals over time. You might have to put it in traction or even in a cast, but it will heal unless there are complications. With inner healing, time doesn't necessarily heal the wound. And our sinful reactions to the pain can cause us to spiral out of the will of God. The primary complication to inner healing is unforgiveness.

With inner healing, we're basically dealing with sinful reactions to hurtful situations. Just because someone hurt us doesn't give us the right to violate Scripture. When we withhold forgiveness, we hinder our inner healing. Praying in tongues can show us what's hindering our healing, help us break through it, and position ourselves for inner healing.

Speaking of Jesus, Psalm 147:3 says, "He heals the brokenhearted and binds up their wounds." Clearly, this is speaking of heart issues, emotional issues. "The Lord is close to all whose hearts are crushed by pain, and he is always ready to restore the repentant one" (Ps. 34:18 TPT).

When we pray in tongues, we are releasing the truth of God, including God's love, His mercy, His compassion, and other truths, and that truth sets us free from the pain. Jesus said, "And you shall know the truth, and the truth shall make you free" (John 8:32). *The Passion Translation* relates, "For if you embrace the truth, it will release true freedom into your lives."

Elliot's Commentary says, "The light of truth dispels the darkness in which lies the stronghold of evil. Sin is the bondage of the powers of the soul, and this bondage is willed because the soul does not see its fearful evil. When it perceives the truth, there comes to it a power which rouses it from its stupor, and strengthens it to break the fetters by which it has been bound."

Who the Son sets free is free indeed, so you are free legally but sometimes people are not free in their living condition. In other words, although freedom is your portion, sometimes you are not experiencing God's freedom in your life. When that happens, you need a truth encounter. Praying in tongues can bring you into that truth encounter.

God sees your inner pain. "The spirit of a man is the lamp of the Lord, searching all the inner depths of his heart" (Prov. 20:27). *The Passion Translation* puts it this way: "The spirit God breathed into man is like a living lamp, a shining light searching into the innermost chamber of our being."

As you pray in the spirit, things may come into the light for which you need to repent or things you need to surrender to Him, including your emotional pain. The Holy Spirit can heal the emotional wounds you didn't even know you had, but He knows and wants to heal you everywhere it hurts.

Prayer

Father, in the name of Jesus, search the inner depths of my soul and heal my innermost being as I pray in tongues. Help me to forgive and surrender the pain to You so I can walk in total freedom.

Get Delivered from Demons

Yes, a Christian can have a demon. In my School of Deliverance, I teach about the many different entry points of demons, from practicing sin to generational curses to trauma inflicted on our souls as children. You can even be demonized in your mother's womb through spirits of rejection or addiction.

Christians cannot be demon-possessed, but demons can oppress our souls and our bodies, even morphing our personalities. Colossians 1:4 tells us, "For we have heard of your faith in Christ Jesus [the leaning of your entire human personality on Him in absolute trust and confidence in His power, wisdom, and goodness] and of the love which you [have and show] for all the saints (God's consecrated ones)" (AMPC).

The Holy Spirit Himself can cast demons out of you as you pray in tongues. Jesus said, "But if I cast out demons with the finger of God, surely the kingdom of God has come upon you" (Luke 11:20). Jesus cast out demons by the power of the Holy Spirit. Jesus is the deliverer and still casts out demons by His power through delegated authority and faith in His name.

The key is you must have forgiven. You cannot be totally set free if you have unforgiveness. The demons will just come right back—and bring more with them. Jesus warned:

> *When an unclean spirit goes out of a man, he goes through dry*
> *places, seeking rest, and finds none. Then he says, "I will return*
> *to my house from which I came." And when he comes, he finds*

it empty, swept, and put in order. Then he goes and takes with him seven other spirits more wicked than himself, and they enter and dwell there; and the last state of that man is worse than the first (Matthew 12:43-45).

All that said, praying in tongues can bring deliverance and help you walk out your deliverance from demons. Demons that are hiding in your soul or in your body may come to the surface and be expelled while praying in tongues. You may know something is wrong with you or may have no idea. But the Holy Spirit knows and is poised to deliver.

The Christ in you can work with the Holy Spirit in you to cast demons out of you by the power of the Holy Spirit as you yield yourself to Him, cry out, and pray in tongues. David wrote, "I sought the Lord, and He heard me, and delivered me from all my fears" (Ps. 34:4). David also wrote, "Call upon Me in the day of trouble; I will deliver you, and you shall glorify Me" (Ps. 50:15).

God has already delivered you from the kingdom of darkness and into the Kingdom of Light, but some darkness may remain in your soul (see Col. 1:13). You don't always automatically get healed and delivered when you are born again. Praying in tongues sets the stage for God to complete the good work He started in You so you can walk in your highest calling, unhindered.

Prayer

Father, in the name of Jesus deliver me from evil. As I pray in tongues, root out the demonic strongholds from my soul. Set me completely free so I can walk in my highest calling.

Unlock Divine Wisdom

Every day, we need wisdom—not wisdom as the world gives it but supernatural wisdom from our all-wise, all-knowing Father in heaven. I dare say we need wisdom more than we realize we need wisdom.

What is wisdom? *Merriam-Webster*'s dictionary defines *wisdom* as "ability to discern inner qualities and relationships, good sense, judgment, a wise attitude, belief, or course of action." I've discerned that common sense isn't so common, so we need to tap into the good sense the Lord gives us, which is wisdom. Praying in tongues unlocks divine wisdom.

James assures us, "If any of you lacks wisdom, let him ask of God, who gives to all liberally and without reproach, and it will be given to him. But let him ask in faith, with no doubting, for he who doubts is like a wave of the sea driven and tossed by the wind" (James 1:5-6). When we pray in tongues, we may be asking for wisdom we don't even know we need.

The Greek word for *wisdom* in James 1:5-6 is *sophia*. According to *The KJV Greek New Testament Lexicon*, it means "wisdom, broad and full of intelligence; used of the knowledge of very diverse matters" and "supreme intelligence, such as belongs to God."

When you pray in tongues with the aim of seeking wisdom, you will find perfect wisdom because you are praying the perfect prayer. Instead of following your own flawed human wisdom, you will tap into the wisdom that is from above. And, even better, you can tap into wisdom that is full of intelligence in very diverse matters—even things of which we have no natural knowledge. We can receive wisdom about situations, circumstances, and problems that we've never encountered before.

James also told us, "But the wisdom that is from above is first pure, then peaceable, gentle, willing to yield, full of mercy and good fruits, without partiality and without hypocrisy" (James 3:17). Many times pastors, friends, or family will give us their wisdom. But the wisdom of man is not always the wisdom of God for our situation. In other words, good advice is not always God's wisdom. What's more, praying in tongues helps us walk in divine wisdom continually. Ephesians 5:15-16 tells us, "See then that you walk circumspectly, not as fools but as wise, redeeming the time, because the days are evil." And Ephesians 5:17 tells us how: "Therefore do not be unwise, but understand what the will of the Lord is."

What I often do is ask for wisdom and then pray in tongues to unlock it so my mind doesn't get in the way. Otherwise, I often find myself asking for wisdom and then trying to work it out through reasoning, pros and cons lists, or my own intellect. God has given us the ability to reason, but we can reason ourselves right out of the wisdom of God.

Proverbs 16:16 tells us, "How much better to get wisdom than gold!" Praying in tongues gives us wisdom beyond our years. Praying in tongues overrides our flawed human wisdom and demonic wisdom that tries to deceive us.

Prayer

Father, in the name of Jesus, pour out Your wisdom upon my life liberally as I pray in tongues. Help me tap into Your perfectly wise counsel rather than the conflicting wisdom of man.

Walk in the Right Place at the Right Time

We all want to be in the right place at the right time. You can be in the right place at the wrong time. You can be in the wrong place at the right time. You can be in the wrong place at the wrong time.

When we pray in tongues with any measure of consistency—and we pay attention to what's going on in us and around us—we are setting ourselves up to be in the right place at the right time. Praying in tongues helps us walk in the right place at the right time.

David wrote these encouraging words in Psalm 37:23: "The steps of a good man are ordered by the Lord, and He delights in his way." The Christian Standard Bible puts it this way: "A person's steps are established by the Lord, and he takes pleasure in his way." And the Good News Translation: "The Lord guides us in the way we should go and protects those who please him."

Of course, God can also order the steps of those who do not pray in tongues, but I know from experience that God has ordered my steps to run into people, to receive blessings and the like through my praying in tongues and walking where He tells me to walk.

By the same token, God orders my steps around demonic attack, perilous accidents, and other circumstances that would delay His will for my life. The psalmist wrote, "Direct my steps by Your word, and let no iniquity have dominion over me" (Ps. 119:133). Pray in tongues with a mind toward the Lord ordering your steps, especially when you are in new territory or need a breakthrough.

I am a big planner. I love to plan exploits, but at times I am sure I have gotten ahead of God. When we pray in tongues, God will override our plans and direct our steps into His will. We see this concept in Proverbs 16:9: "A man's heart plans his way, but the Lord directs his steps."

The Lord can order your steps to a place without your natural awareness. You just decide to go a different way home and end up getting there much faster, so you catch your neighbor—whom you almost never see—and find the information you needed, etc. Jeremiah 10:23 promises, "O Lord, I know the way of man is not in himself; it is not in man who walks to direct his own steps."

Again, God can order even the steps of the wicked, but I know praying in tongues causes us, sometimes even without realizing it, to go a certain direction. We can see later how God's hand was in it, ordering our steps. Psalm 32:8 reveals, "I will instruct you and teach you in the way you should go; I will guide you with My eye."

Prayer

Father, in the name of Jesus, as I pray in tongues will You order and reorder my steps so I can walk in Your way? Will You guide me with Your eye to the places You've called me to walk?

Tap into
the Mind of Christ

You're probably familiar with First Corinthians 2:16: "For 'who has known the mind of the Lord that he may instruct Him?' But we have the mind of Christ." Like you, I've read this Scripture innumerable times—but I had never looked into the deeper meaning of what the verse is saying.

The Greek word for *mind* in this verse is *nubo*. According to *The KJV New Testament Greek Lexicon*, it means "reason in the narrower sense, as the capacity for spiritual truth, the higher powers of the soul, the faculty of perceiving divine things, of recognizing goodness and of hating evil."

Praying in tongues helps us tap into Christ's way of reasoning and thinking. Although His thoughts are higher than our thoughts, we can tap into His higher thoughts when we pray in tongues.

Nubo also means "the power of considering and judging soberly, calmly and impartially," and "a particular mode of thinking and judging, i.e. thoughts, feelings, purposes, desires." Praying in tongues helps us tap into the power to think and feel the way Christ thinks and feels. It helps us understand His purposes and desires.

The Amplified Classic version of First Corinthians 2:16 says, "For who has known or understood the mind (the counsels and purposes) of the Lord so as to guide and instruct Him and give Him knowledge? But we have the mind of Christ (the Messiah) and do hold the thoughts (feelings and purposes) of His heart."

As born-again citizens of the Kingdom of God with covenant benefits galore, we have the legal right to request access to the mind of Christ and the thoughts, feelings, and purposes of His heart. Of course, we can pray in our natural language and ask God what He's thinking. But praying in tongues gives us that line into things we don't know to ask for.

The Contemporary English Version of this verse reads, "The Scriptures ask, 'Has anyone ever known the thoughts of the Lord or given him advice?' But we understand what Christ is thinking."

You may be thinking, "No, I don't understand what He's thinking." When you pray in tongues, it renews your mind and helps you become more aware about what God is thinking in any given situation. IHOPKC director Mike Bickle taught me to pray, "Lord let me think what You think and feel what You feel about...." When I pray that and then pray in tongues, the mind of Christ is often revealed.

The Passion Translation puts it this way: "For who has ever intimately known the mind of the Lord Yahweh well enough to become his counselor? Christ has, and we possess Christ's perceptions." I like that. We possess Christ's perceptions. If you are not sure if something is your perception or Christ's perception, pray in tongues.

Finally, *The Message* offers, "Spiritually alive, we have access to everything God's Spirit is doing, and can't be judged by unspiritual critics. Isaiah's question, 'Is there anyone around who knows God's Spirit, anyone who knows what he is doing?' has been answered: Christ knows, and we have Christ's Spirit."

Are you ready to tap into the mind of Christ?

Prayer

Father, in the name of Jesus, I want to get out of my head and into Yours. As I pray in tongues, would You give me insight into Your higher thoughts? Would You give me access to Your perfect mind?

Move from Glory to Glory

Glory to glory is your portion. You can move from glory to glory little by little—and you will if you are pursuing Christ—or you can accelerate your glory shifts by praying in tongues. To some measure, the glory growth depends on you.

Paul wrote these inspiring words in Second Corinthians 3:18, "But we all, with unveiled face, beholding as in a mirror the glory of the Lord, are being transformed into the same image from glory to glory, just as by the Spirit of the Lord."

So what is this glory? According to *The KJV New Testament Greek Lexicon, glory* means, "the kingly majesty which belongs to Him as supreme ruler, majesty in the sense of the absolute perfection of the deity." I want this glory! Praying in tongues brings us into these glories through the transforming power of the Holy Spirit.

The New International Version translates Second Corinthians 3:18 this way: "And we all, who with unveiled faces contemplate the Lord's glory, are being transformed into his image with ever-increasing glory, which comes from the Lord, who is the Spirit."

So we are being incrementally refined and shaped into the image of Christ as we pray in tongues. There are different degrees of glory. Your level of glory is different than my level of glory. But our glory is influenced, in part, by how much we yield our tongues to the Holy Spirit's utterance.

The Contemporary English Version shares it this way: "So our faces are not covered. They show the bright glory of the Lord, as the Lord's Spirit makes us more and more like our glorious Lord."

Other definitions of *glory* from the Greek word are, "the absolutely perfect inward or personal excellency of Christ" and "most glorious condition, most exalted state" and "that condition with God the Father in heaven to which Christ was raised after he had achieved his work on earth." I want that glory, so I will pray in tongues all the more.

The New Living Translation relates, "So all of us who have had that veil removed can see and reflect the glory of the Lord. And the Lord— who is the Spirit—makes us more and more like him as we are changed into his glorious image." We are supposed to reflect His glory. We reflect more glory when we pray in tongues.

The Message says, "And so we are transfigured much like the Messiah, our lives gradually becoming brighter and more beautiful as God enters our lives and we become like him." Another definition of *glory* is "the glorious condition of blessedness into which is appointed and promised that true Christians shall enter after their Savior's return from heaven." I want this ultimate glory, so I will pray in tongues until He returns! What about you?

Prayer

Father, in the name of Jesus, I want to accelerate my glory shifts. As I pray in tongues, will You bring me into new glory, and then another and another. Would You help me continue to grow in the knowledge of Your glory?

Supercharge
Your Dream Life

Have you ever spoken in tongues in a dream? That could signify that you are praying in tongues so much that it's infiltrated your dream life—and praying in tongues can certainly supercharge your dream life.

Indeed, there's a direct connection in Scripture to the outpouring of the Holy Spirit and prophetic dreams. Acts 2:17 recounts this transformational event on the Day of Pentecost: "And it shall come to pass in the last days, says God, that I will pour out of My Spirit on all flesh; your sons and your daughters shall prophesy, your young men shall see visions, your old men shall dream dreams."

Remember, praying in tongues opens up revelation and unlocks mysteries. Sometimes God brings that revelation to you through your dreams. Job unpacked this truth:

> *For God may speak in one way, or in another, yet man does not perceive it. In a dream, in a vision of the night, when deep sleep falls upon men, while slumbering on their beds, then He opens the ears of men, and seals their instruction* (Job 33:14-16).

The Passion Translation offers the verses in Acts this way: "This is what I will do in the last days—I will pour out my Spirit on everybody and cause your sons and daughters to prophesy, and your young men will see visions, and your old men will experience dreams from God."

Sometimes God speaks to us in dreams because we are not hearing Him while we're awake. We're too concerned about too many things, so He communicates with us while He has our undivided attention—in our sleep. When we pray in tongues, we are positioning ourselves for more dream revelation. While you can't make God give you a dream or make God speak to you, praying in tongues makes us more sensitive to His voice when He does speak—no matter how He speaks.

The Amplified Classic version says, "dream [divinely suggested] dreams." We're all dreaming more than we remember. Praying in tongues when you wake up can also help you remember your divinely suggested dreams. John 14:26 tells us the Holy Spirit can remind us of what Jesus said. Since praying in tongues is praying the perfect prayer, praying in tongues can bring God's will to pass in the area of receiving and remembering dreams.

God spoke to people in dreams all throughout the Old and New Testament and in the early chapters of the New Testament. God has not stopped bringing prophetic revelation through dreams. We sleep, on average, eight hours a night. Don't you think God wants to speak to us in our dreams? Praying in tongues can open up your dream world at new levels.

Also consider this: If you used to dream but stopped dreaming, praying in tongues can open this dimension back up to you, if God wills. Sometimes, traumas or fears block our will to dream, or we've asked God to shut down dreams. Praying in tongues can break through the hinderances.

Prayer

Father, in the name of Jesus, would You supercharge my dream life as I pray in tongues? Would You help me remember the prophetic dreams You share with me in my sleep?

Interpret Your Own Dreams

God speaks to us in dreams more than we may realize. And, as I said previously, many people have prophetic dreams but they don't remember them. Praying in tongues can help us remember the dreams we know we had but can't remember, and it can also help us interpret divine dreams we receive.

I would be remiss if I didn't warn you that not every dream is from God. Some teachers are insisting every dream is divine, but that's an error. Dreams can come from three main sources: 1) your carnal nature (eating too late, taking medicine, having too many cares in your mind, depression, etc.); 2) the enemy (night terrors, nightmares, and other nocturnal attacks); and 3) God.

So we need to judge dreams before we interpret them. Once we've determined a dream is divine, we must press in to understand all that God is saying. Proverbs 25:2 tells us plainly: "It is the glory of God to conceal a matter, but the glory of kings is to search out a matter."

You can search it out through Bible study—the better you understand the Word of God, the easier it is to interpret what He is saying while you sleep. You can also search out your dreams through meditating on them and prayer. Praying in tongues is one way to receive revelation.

The Contemporary English Version puts the verse this way: "God is praised for being mysterious; rulers are praised for explaining mysteries."

Remember, praying in tongues unlocks mysteries—and some of God's mysteries are related in your dream life.

The Passion Translation relates: "God conceals the revelation of his word in the hiding place of his glory. But the honor of kings is revealed by how they thoroughly search out the deeper meaning of all that God says." The Holy Spirit knows everything. Praying in tongues can help you get a revelation on the deeper meaning of your dreams. It can just "come to you."

Paul the apostle shared some wisdom in First Corinthians 2:13, "These things we also speak, not in words which man's wisdom teaches but which the Holy Spirit teaches, comparing spiritual things with spiritual." The Holy Spirit can teach us the spiritual meaning of our dreams, which are often filled with symbols, colors, numbers, and metaphors. While dreams can be literal, they are more often parabolic and symbolic. Praying in tongues can unlock the spiritual truths in your dreams.

I would caution you not to go to the internet to discover the meanings of your dreams. That can lead you into error and New Age practices. When the baker and the butler told Joseph their dreams while they were together in prison, hoping for an interpretation, the prophet was quick to say, "Do not interpretations belong to God?" (Gen. 40:8).

Remember, the interpretation belongs to God. He knows it. He knows everything. Sometimes He doesn't let you know the interpretation immediately. But praying in tongues will prime the pump for the discovery of God's interpretation. Don't give up.

Prayer

Father, in the name of Jesus, would You give me the interpretation of my dreams? As I pray in tongues, would You show me the meaning of what You showed me while I was asleep?

More Sensitive to Holy Spirit's Conviction

The Holy Spirit is the one who convicts—and we should welcome His loving conviction. The enemy condemns, but the Holy Spirit convicts. When you understand the love of God, you will be able to tell the difference, rejecting condemnation and appreciating Holy Spirit's conviction.

Jesus said in John 16:8, "And when He has come, He will convict the world of sin, and of righteousness, and of judgment." Praying in tongues makes you more sensitive to the Holy Spirit's discipline, which is critical. The Lord disciplines those He loves (see Heb. 12:6). Receiving conviction means we can repent quickly and get back in line. Praying in tongues makes us more sensitive to the Holy Spirit's conviction.

Now, the Greek word for *convict* is *elegcho*. According to *The KJV New Testament Greek Lexicon* it means "to convict, refute, confute, generally with a suggestion of shame of the person convicted, by conviction to bring to the light, to expose, to find fault with, correct, chasten, to punish." Praying in tongues makes you more sensitive to grieving the Holy Spirit through sins of omission and sins of commission.

Even if you don't know what the Word of God commands in a given situation, the Holy Spirit knows the Word intimately and can convict you before you step into a sin, or use conviction to pull you into repentance. That's how good He is. We should embrace the concept of godly sorrow, but never demonic shame. God loves you.

The Contemporary English Version puts John 16:8 this way: "The Spirit will come and show the people of this world the truth about sin and God's justice and the judgment." We need to see the truth about our sin so we can turn away from it. Praying in tongues makes it easier for us to see when we've missed the mark.

The Aramaic Bible in Plain English translates the verse like this: "And when he comes, he will correct the world concerning sin and concerning righteousness and concerning judgment." Praying in tongues opens our hearts to receive the Holy Spirit's gentle correction so we don't stray too far away from His loving protection.

Many people like to play Holy Ghost Junior, judging and criticizing us. Likewise, the enemy wants us to wallow in guilt, shame, and condemnation. The Holy Spirit exposes our sin to us so we can repent privately and come back into perfect alignment with His heart. Then, the enemy has no right to attack us.

The Holy Spirit is a gentleman. He doesn't come in like a bulldozer or an angry father with a belt trying to catch you and whip you. That's not His nature. It's not how He moves. His conviction is an expression of His love, wooing you back to the Father's heart. It's the kindness of God that leads us to repentance.

The Passion Translation says, "And when he comes, he will expose sin and prove that the world is wrong about God's righteousness and his judgments."

Sometimes we don't know we're doing something wrong because we're deceived. Perhaps we were taught wrong or weren't taught at all. Praying in tongues helps us to see what we didn't see before.

Prayer

Father, in the name of Jesus, please convict me when I sin—
and even before I sin. As I pray in tongues, would You make
me all the more sensitive to Your gentle conviction?

Bear Witness
to Your Identity

Bearing witness to the truth is part of the Holy Spirit's ministry in our spirit. We need to bear witness to who we are in Christ, but we also need to bear witness to the truth about others.

In Romans 8:16 Paul wrote, "The Spirit Himself testifies with our spirit that we are children of God" (NASB). This is in the field of discernment, but it goes beyond that because praying in tongues helps you receive the truth about who you are in Christ. And that's vital in to your intimacy with God, your ability to withstand trials and tribulation, and your success in spiritual warfare.

The New Living Translation puts it this way: "For his Spirit joins with our spirit to affirm that we are God's children." Too many Christians are not deeply rooted in their identity in God's Kingdom. Praying in tongues helps us see who we really are—and everything changes for the better when you know who you are.

Of course, you can learn who you are in Christ by reading the Word, but the Holy Spirit drives this down deep when you pray in tongues. Indeed, when you pray in tongues you are watering the seed of the Word of truth about who you are and renewing your mind to this reality.

Think of a courtroom wherein satan, the accuser of the brethren, has put your salvation on trial because you sinned and fell short of God's glory. Maybe you are in a season of lukewarmness or even backsliding.

We need the Holy Spirit's encouragement that we are children of God and can return to Him without condemnation.

When I first got saved, I was not baptized in the Holy Spirit. I thought every time I made a mistake, I had to get saved all over again. If I said, did, or thought anything wrong, I thought I would go to hell if I died. Of course, that idea came from the enemy. So, I said the sinner's prayer over and over. Once I got baptized in the Holy Spirit, all that stopped. The Holy Spirit testified within my spirit that I am a child of God.

The Amplified Classic translates Romans 8:16 this way: "The Spirit Himself [thus] testifies together with our own spirit, [assuring us] that we are children of God."

Of course, the Holy Spirit also testifies to your spirit so you can discern other truths in the Word. The more you pray in the Spirit, the easier it will be for you to know if a preacher is preaching the truth.

In John 16:13, Jesus said the Holy Spirt is the spirit of truth and He will lead us and guide us into all truth. All means all.

Prayer

Father, in the name of Jesus, teach me who I really am. As I pray in tongues, root deeply within me a revelation of my identity so I can walk not just as a child of God but a mature son of God.

Grace to Obey God

Someone once asked Korea's David Yonggi Cho how he built such a massive ministry. (He has millions of members in his church.) His answer: "I pray. I obey." Those are words to live by. The reality is none of us are fully obedient. We need the Holy Sprit's help to obey. Praying in tongues helps us tap into the grace of obedience.

This is critical, as Jesus said, "If you love Me you will keep My commandments" (see John 14:15). That's pretty heavy. Think about this for a minute. We display our love for Jesus through agreeing with and executing His command for our lives.

Again, we won't get it perfect all the time. We all sin and fall short of the glory of God (see Rom. 3:23). But we can set our heart toward one-hundredfold obedience. Praying in tongues strengthens you to obey God. When you pray in tongues with a heart toward obedience, it empowers you to obey God.

Jesus went on to say in Luke 6:46, "But why do you call Me 'Lord, Lord,' and not do the things which I say?" And in Matthew 7:21 Jesus said, "Not everyone who says to Me, 'Lord, Lord,' shall enter the kingdom of heaven, but he who does the will of My Father in heaven." Again, this is heavy.

When Saul disobeyed the Lord's command to wipe out the Amalekites completely, he made excuses for his sin. The prophet Samuel told him, "Behold, to obey is better than sacrifice, and to heed than the fat of rams" (1 Sam. 15:22). When we tap into the grace of obedience the Holy Spirit helps us submit to God, whose commandments are not burdensome (see 1 John 5:3).

Jesus had more to say about obedience: "If anyone loves Me, he will keep My word; and My Father will love him, and We will come to him and make Our home with him" (John 14:23). This is one of the benefits of obedience, and there are many.

Consider Isaiah 1:19: "If you are willing and obedient, you shall eat the good of the land." James 4:7 tells us, "Therefore submit to God. Resist the devil and he will flee from you." Finally, consider Ezekiel 36:26-27:

> *I will give you a new heart and put a new spirit within you; I will take the heart of stone out of your flesh and give you a heart of flesh. I will put My Spirit within you and cause you to walk in My statutes, and you will keep My judgments and do them.*

The implication here is when we are born again, we have the will and the strength through the power of the Holy Spirit who dwells within us to obey God. Although the righteous man falls seven times, he gets back up again (see Prov. 24:16).

God wouldn't give us commands without the power to obey. His commandments are not burdensome because of grace. When you pray in tongues, it activates a greater desire and ability to obey God. It helps us to demonstrate our love for Jesus through submission to His will. It helps us be like Cho—to pray and obey.

Prayer

Father, in the name of Jesus, I want to comprehend Your Word. I want to walk in Your understanding of the Word. Please sharpen my understanding as I pray in tongues.

BENEFIT 55

Abound in Hope

God is a God of hope. It's part of the strength of His character. He sees your end from the beginning, even when everything that can go wrong in your life is going wrong—and even when you miss the mark. Praying in tongues helps us to abound in God's hope.

Romans 15:13 tells us, "Now may the God of hope fill you with all joy and peace in believing, that you may abound in hope by the power of the Holy Spirit." Praying in tongues helps you abound in hope by rooting out doubt.

Even in judgment, even in dire circumstances, even in life and death situations, God remains a God of hope. Hope is vital because faith is the substance of things hoped for (see Heb. 11:1). If the enemy can steal your hope, he can steal your faith. Praying in tongues helps you abound in hope by rooting out doubt.

The Passion Translation of Romans 15:13 says, "Now may God, the fountain of hope, fill you to overflowing with uncontainable joy and perfect peace as you trust in him. And may the power of the Holy Spirit continually surround your life with his super-abundance until you radiate with hope!"

God's goodness and love should inspire hope in us. If God is a fountain of hope, and He is, and rivers of living water flow through your belly when you are filled with the Holy Spirit, and they do, then wouldn't it make sense that praying in tongues will cause hope to bubble up in your spirit? Makes perfect sense to me. When we radiate hope, we can bring hope to a hopeless world. We can overflow with hope.

The Amplified Classic relates Romans 15:13 like this: "May the God of your hope so fill you with all joy and peace in believing [through the experience of your faith] that by the power of the Holy Spirit you may abound and be overflowing (bubbling over) with hope."

There are clear promises for those who tap into God's hope. Isaiah 40:31 tells us those who hope in the Lord will renew their strength. And Psalm 25:2 tells us if we hope in the Lord we will never be put to shame. Praying in tongues positions us to abound in this hope.

The New Living Translation of Romans 15:13 tells us, "I pray that God, the source of hope, will fill you completely with joy and peace because you trust in him. Then you will overflow with confident hope through the power of the Holy Spirit."

God is the source of all hope. Praying in tongues can help you tap into that source directly. Waiting can create hopelessness and hope deferred makes the heart sick, but we can pray in the spirit and tap into a wellspring of hope.

No matter what you are going through, God has a future and a hope for you (see Jer. 29:11). Praying in tongues helps us hope for what we do not see (see Rom. 8:25).

Prayer

Father, in the name of Jesus, help me combat the enemy's hopeless lies with Your abounding hope as I pray in tongues. Root out of me any hopelessness that hinders my faith to stand on Your words of hope.

Unlock the Spirit of Understanding

The Bible has plenty to say about understanding, which is critical as we walk as citizens of the Kingdom in a world that's not our home (see Heb. 13:14). We need Holy Spirit comprehension and interpretation of the Word and the world around us.

You can get understanding by both the Word and the Spirit. Praying in the spirit unlocks the spirit of understanding, which is one of the seven spirits of God mentioned in Isaiah 11. The seven spirits of God reality is a mystery, just as the Trinity—the three in one God—is a mystery. We don't have to understand this mystery to tap into the benefits of the Holy Spirit's ministry.

Isaiah 11:2 speaks of the spirit of understanding. Praying in tongues unlocks the spirit of understanding. Praying in tongues will help us tap into the understanding that we need to pray rightly, move rightly, think rightly, to make decisions rightly, and so on. Praying in tongues also helps us understand others, which is important to healthy relationships.

Psalm 119:130 promises, "The entrance of Your words gives light; it gives understanding to the simple." I'm all for a college education, but if you have understanding of the Word of God you are positioned to make better choices than someone who has a university degree without Word knowledge.

Paul charged his spiritual son Timothy to, "Consider what I say, and may the Lord give you understanding in all things" (2 Tim. 2:7). When you consider the Word and pray in tongues, understanding comes into the deep things of God.

When Jesus walked with His disciples, "He opened their understanding, that they might comprehend the Scriptures" (Luke 24:45). Think about that. Jesus, the Word made flesh, opened the eyes of hearts to understand what God was saying. He can do the same for us.

David prayed this: "Give me understanding, and I shall keep Your law; indeed, I shall observe it with my whole heart" (Ps. 119:34). Praying in tongues while reading the Word, which takes some practice, supercharges your reception of light. Remember, your tongues are not formulated in your natural mind, so you can pray in tongues and read at the same time.

Solomon shared this wisdom in Proverbs 2:2, "Apply your heart to understanding." You can apply your heart to understand a verse of Scripture or a situation by praying in tongues. The Holy Spirit lives in your heart, so when you pray in tongues you are applying your heart to understanding.

There are many benefits to gaining understanding. Proverbs 17:27 relates, "And a man of understanding is of a calm spirit." Praying in tongues can unlock understanding so you can react to situations with a cool spirit. Proverbs 2:11 promises, "Understanding will keep you." And Proverbs 3:13 shares, "Happy is the man who finds wisdom, and the man who gains understanding."

Proverbs 3:5 admonishes: "Trust in the Lord with all your heart, and lean not on your own understanding." One way we demonstrate trust in the Holy Spirit and unlock His understanding rather than leaning on our own understanding is by praying in tongues.

Prayer

Father, in the name of Jesus, I need understanding in many areas. As I pray in tongues, would You give me Your understanding about the Word, about challenges I face, and about the issues of life?

Receive Divine Wisdom

We all need wisdom. Indeed, praying for wisdom should be a serious endeavor. That's because if you aren't desperate for wisdom in this season there is surely coming a time when you will crave its rewards. Praying in tongues helps you receive divine wisdom.

Proverbs 16:16 tells us, "How much better to get wisdom than gold!" Divine wisdom is better than the world's wisdom. God's wisdom is unmatchable and perfect, with the ability to deliver you from trouble—even trouble you brought upon yourself.

What is wisdom? *Merriam-Webster*'s dictionary defines *wisdom* as "ability to discern inner qualities and relationships, good sense, judgment, a wise attitude, belief, or course of action." You might say it this way: wisdom is a God-given ability to help shape our attitudes, words, beliefs, and actions.

James, the apostle of practical faith, offers this instruction: "If any of you lacks wisdom, let him ask of God, who gives to all liberally and without reproach, and it will be given to him. But let him ask in faith, with no doubting, for he who doubts is like a wave of the sea driven and tossed by the wind" (James 1:5-6). Praying in the spirit unlocks this wisdom.

The Greek word for *wisdom* in this verse is *sophia*. According to *The KJV Greek New Testament Lexicon*, *sophia* means "wisdom, broad and full of intelligence; used of the knowledge of very diverse matters" and "supreme intelligence, such as belongs to God."

When you have divine wisdom, you're tapping into prophetic intelligence and diverse knowledge about issues you know nothing about in the natural. You can receive divine wisdom about circumstances, situations, and problems you've never encountered before. You may get wisdom from a wise person, but it doesn't mean they are offering divine wisdom.

When you pray in tongues with the aim of seeking wisdom, you will find wisdom because you are praying the perfect prayer and the Holy Spirit knows what's in the mind of the Father. Instead of following your own flawed human wisdom, you will tap into the wisdom that is from above.

James wrote these wise words to help us discern divine wisdom from human or demonic wisdom: "But the wisdom that is from above is first pure, then peaceable, gentle, willing to yield, full of mercy and good fruits, without partiality and without hypocrisy" (James 3:17).

This is a critical matter. Ephesians 5:17 commands us to walk in wisdom: "Therefore do not be unwise, but understand what the will of the Lord is." We can't always find the wisdom we need in our minds or from past experience, but the good news is praying in tongues gives us wisdom beyond our years.

Praying in tongues also helps us walk in wisdom continually so we don't have to wait for a critical moment to cry out for sudden wisdom. "See then that you walk circumspectly, not as fools but as wise, redeeming the time, because the days are evil" (Eph. 5:15-16).

Prayer

Father, in the name of Jesus, I need Your pure, gentle, and peaceable wisdom more than I realize. Please pour out Your wisdom liberally as I pray in tongues. Please, flood my heart with wisdom from above.

Fast-Track Your Discernment

D o you need more discernment? We all do. The Bible tells us over and over again to discern, and this skill is sorely lacking in the Body of Christ. Praying in tongues makes you more naturally and spiritually discerning over time.

See, there's the gift of discerning of spirits and then there's discernment, which is different. Discerning of spirits is a Holy Spirit gift and some believers flow in this without even trying. Natural discernment is something in which we all must grow. Discernment is separating good from evil. Praying in tongues will help you grow in both regards.

The need for discernment is critical across the board. John the beloved told us to discern spirits in First John 4:1: "Beloved, do not believe every spirit, but test the spirits, whether they are of God; because many false prophets have gone out into the world." Praying in tongues helps us discern true and false prophets.

Then there's John 7:24, which tells us, "Do not judge according to appearance, but judge with righteous judgment." Praying in tongues helps us make a righteous judgment—or to discern by the Holy Spirit. We don't want to be critical or judgmental of people. We want to discern. Praying in tongues can root out the suspicion, criticism, and judgmental attitudes so we can discern more accurately.

Finally, First Thessalonians 5:21 says, "Test all things; hold fast what is good." Remember, discernment is separating good from evil. Praying in tongues helps you discern not just what the enemy is doing but also what God is doing in your life or in an atmosphere.

When we pray in tongues, we become more spiritually discerning over time. It's part of the edification process. We grow little by little and then have a noticeable breakthrough. Paul made clear in First Corinthians 2:14, "But the natural man does not receive the things of the Spirit of God, for they are foolishness to him; nor can he know them, because they are spiritually discerned."

We grow our spiritual discernment by exercising it, but praying in tongues can accelerate the growth of our discernment muscles. Hebrews 5:14 tells us, "But solid food belongs to those who are of full age, that is, those who by reason of use have their senses exercised to discern both good and evil."

We need to discern the will of God. Romans 12:2 relates, "Do not be conformed to this world, but be transformed by the renewal of your mind, that by testing you may discern what is the will of God, what is good and acceptable and perfect" (ESV). Praying in tongues helps us discern the will of God.

Paul prayed for His disciples to grow in discernment in an apostolic prayer found in Philippians 1:9-10, "And this I pray, that your love may abound still more and more in knowledge and all discernment, that you may approve the things that are excellent, that you may be sincere and without offense till the day of Christ."

Prayer

Father, in the name of Jesus, I need to grow in spiritual and natural discernment. Would You help me deepen my discernment as I pray in tongues? Root out of me biases and anything else that hinders my discernment.

Push Back Darkness

When you are in a spiritual battle, it's ultimately a battle between darkness and light. In spiritual warfare, darkness is trying to encroach on God's light over your life—whether in your physical body, your finances, your family, your friendships, your career, or your ministry. The enemy wants to cast a demonic shadow over every aspect of your life.

When you pray in tongues, you are releasing spiritual light. You are releasing rivers of living water—rivers of living light. I believe when we pray in tongues, we are lit up in the spirit. When we pray in tongues, we are hiding in the light. Jesus said John the Baptist burned and shone and people enjoyed his light (see John 5:35).

When we pray in tongues, the enemy does not like to come near us because God's light blinds him. "And the light shines in the darkness, and the darkness did not comprehend it" (John 1:5). *The Passion Translation* says, "And this Light never fails to shine through darkness—Light that darkness could not overcome!"

Jesus spoke of this light—and described Himself as light: "I am the light of the world. He who follows Me shall not walk in darkness, but have the light of life" (John 8:12). If you are in Christ, and you are, then you are in the light.

But you still have to choose to follow Him every day. When you follow Him, you will not walk in darkness, you will not fall into the enemy's trap. Praying in tongues helps you follow the light.

Paul explained a glorious truth: "For you were once darkness, but now you are light in the Lord. Walk as children of light" (Eph. 5:8). The enemy doesn't know what to do with a believer who is walking in the light—walking in the Spirit. He can't touch you. You are immune to his darkness. Praying in tongues helps us walk as children of light so that darkness cannot settle around us.

Paul also told us this: "The night is far spent, the day is at hand. Therefore let us cast off the works of darkness, and let us put on the armor of light" (Rom. 13:12). Catch that—the armor of light. I believe when we pray in tongues, we're putting on our armor of light. The enemy cannot penetrate the armor of light!

The Greek word for *light* in Romans 13:12 is *phoc*. It means, "a heavenly light such as surrounds angels when they appear on earth" and "of truth and its knowledge, together with the spiritual purity associated with it."

Matthew Henry's Commentary says, "Observe what we must put on; how we should dress our souls. Put on the armour of light. A Christian must reckon himself undressed, if unarmed. The graces of the Spirit are this armour, to secure the soul from Satan's temptations, and the assaults of this present evil world."

Prayer

Father, in the name of Jesus, thank You for the armor of light. As I pray in tongues, would You blind the enemy of my soul with Your everlasting light? Would You hide me in Your light?

Shift Spiritual Atmospheres

You carry the Kingdom of God. The Kingdom of God is within you (see Luke 17:21). The Kingdom of God is not on the other side of Pluto. God is everywhere and He is in you. *The Passion Translation* of Luke 17:21 puts it this way: "The kingdom is not discovered in one place or another, for God's kingdom realm is already expanding within some of you."

Because the Kingdom of God is with you, you are a glory carrier, a Kingdom releaser, a climate changer, and an atmosphere shifter. *Merriam-Webster*'s dictionary defines this aspect of an atmosphere as "a surrounding influence or environment." Praying in tongues helps you discern and shift the surrounding influence in a room or a region to bring it in line with God's will.

Just as when you make intercession, decree a thing, or worship, you can shift atmospheres when you pray in tongues because you are yielding to the Holy Spirit within you to accomplish His will around you.

The Amplified Classic translation of Luke 17:21 expands on the truth: "For behold, the kingdom of God is within you [in your hearts] and among you [surrounding you]." When you walk into a room, the Kingdom is not only in you but surrounding you. The Kingdom goes with you. You release the Kingdom at greater measure when you pray in tongues.

I'm not talking about only about a natural atmosphere, although we do see prophets taking authority over atmospheres in the Bible. Elijah said there would be no rain and there was no rain. Elijah prayed for rain and rain came. Jesus rebuked the wind and spoke to the storm and it settled. I believe we can change natural atmospheres, such as pushing back hurricanes, by praying in tongues.

But we can also change the unseen atmosphere. Praying in tongues may invite angels into the room, send devils packing, attract the overwhelming presence of God, and more.

Have you ever walked into a room and sensed the strife? Have you ever walked in a room and sensed depression? Rather than coming into agreement with or submitting to a foul atmosphere, you can take authority over the demon powers and shift the atmosphere by praying in tongues.

When you pray in tongues your prayers are releasing God's will into that atmosphere through a perfect prayer. By praying in tongues you are releasing the Kingdom of God into an atmosphere—God's light that dispels darkness.

Many times there's nothing you can say in your natural language to cut strife or help someone through depression, but if you pray in tongues the Holy Spirit can move upon their hearts. Praying in tongues can release the Holy Spirit to minister to them so they snap out of the fog and peace comes.

You can also change the atmosphere in your home. If people are living with you who are in sin or consuming media that leaves the atmosphere funky, praying in tongues can change the climate in your dwelling.

Prayer

Father, in the name of Jesus, help me catch this revelation of being an atmosphere shifter. As I pray in tongues, help me discern and, when necessary, work through me to shift spiritual atmospheres and climates according to Your will.

Accelerate Mind Renewal

Our minds need to be renewed—and it's a lifelong process. The enemy sows seeds in our souls before we're born again—and sometimes even after we know the Lord. We have wrong thoughts and wrong beliefs about who we are, who He is, what the Bible says, and more. Praying in tongues helps us obey Romans 12:2.

Paul wrote: "And do not be conformed to this world, but be transformed by the renewing of your mind, that you may prove what is that good and acceptable and perfect will of God." I believe God's will is at the same time good, acceptable, and perfect, and praying in tongues helps us renew our mind to His will.

The Greek word for *renewing* in that verse is *anakainosis*. According to *The KJV New Testament Greek Lexicon*, it means "a renewal, renovation, complete change for the better." And *Merriam-Webster*'s dictionary defines *renew* as, "to make like new: restore to freshness, vigor, or perfection and to become new or as new."

Before we were born we did not have a sin nature because we were spirits. God knew us even before we were in our mother's womb (see Jer. 1:5). When we were born into this world, we were born into sin. By default, we were conditioned to the ways of the world and our minds were influenced by the spirit of the world. When we get born again, we are translated out of the kingdom of darkness into the Kingdom of light, but our minds still need to be renovated.

In addition to meditating on the Word, praying in tongues helps renew your mind because the Holy Spirit is the change agent. The enemy works for years to build strongholds in our minds, and when we pray in tongues the Holy Spirit is working to tear down those strongholds and replace them with truth that sets you free.

The Bible tells us in Philippians 4:8, "Finally, brethren, whatever things are true, whatever things are noble, whatever things are just, whatever things are pure, whatever things are lovely, whatever things are of good report, if there is any virtue and if there is anything praiseworthy—meditate on these things."

If we are not thinking on these things we need to do Ephesians 4:23, "and be renewed in the spirit of your mind." Praying in tongues helps you to be renewed in the spirit of your mind so you can avoid thinking harmful thoughts and think Philippians thoughts.

Psalm 119:11 tells us, "Your word I have hidden in my heart, that I might not sin against You." If the Word were a stake in the ground, praying in tongues would be like a mallet driving the Word deeper into the ground of your heart.

In John 17:17, Jesus prayed for us, saying: "Sanctify them by Your truth. Your word is truth." I believe when we pray in tongues and read the Word, or pray in tongues before or after reading the Word, it prepares our hearts and cements or seals the Word in our heart.

Prayer

Father, in the name of Jesus, as I pray in tongues would You root out enemy strongholds in my mind? Would You renew my mind to Your good, acceptable and perfect will?

Pass God's Tests

Some people don't believe God gives us tests—but He does. And the teacher is often quiet during the test. Don't believe me? Let's look at the Scripture.

Psalm 11:5 tells us plainly, "The Lord tests the righteous, but the wicked and the one who loves violence His soul hates." Proverbs 17:3 reveals, "The refining pot is for silver and the furnace for gold, but the Lord tests the hearts."

God tests us before He promotes us so we can see what's in us that's holding us back from our highest calling. He shows us so we can repent and cooperate with His grace to overcome what hinders our walk. Praying in tongues helps us pass God's tests.

Peter the apostle told us, "the genuineness of your faith, being much more precious than gold that perishes, though it is tested by fire, may be found to praise, honor, and glory at the revelation of Jesus Christ" (1 Pet. 1:7). And Psalm 66:10 says, "For You, O God, have tested us; You have refined us as silver is refined."

The Hebrew word for *test* in this verse is *bachan*. According to *The KJV Old Testament Hebrew Lexicon*, it means "to examine, try, prove, scrutinize, test, and put on trial." Praying in tongues helps prepare us for the test and helps us make it to the end of the test with an A++.

Peter also offered these sobering words in First Peter 4:12-16:

Beloved, do not think it strange concerning the fiery trial which is to try you, as though some strange thing happened to you; but rejoice to the extent that you partake of Christ's sufferings, that when His glory is revealed, you may also be glad with exceeding joy. If you are reproached for the name of Christ, blessed are you, for the Spirit of glory and of God rests upon you. On their part He is blasphemed, but on your part He is glorified. But let none of you suffer as a murderer, a thief, an evildoer, or as a busybody in other people's matters. Yet if anyone suffers as a Christian, let him not be ashamed, but let him glorify God in this matter.

Praying in tongues helps us understand what is happening in the test so we suffer with dignity rather than with murmuring and complaining. Praying in tongues also helps us follow James' advice in James 1:2-3, "My brethren, count it all joy when you fall into various trials, knowing that the testing of your faith produces patience." Praying in tongues helps us to be more joyful in the trial because we get the revelation of the big picture and how the outcome will benefit us in the long run.

The outcome is golden. Job, who was severely tested, assures us of this: "But He knows the way that I take; when He has tested me, I shall come forth as gold" (Job 23:10). Job didn't have the benefit of praying in tongues during his earth-shattering trial, but you do. So, when you are going through a test, yield your tongue to the Holy Spirit and pray.

Prayer

Father, in the name of Jesus, when I am being tested and tried would You remind me to pray in tongues? And, as I yield my tongue to You, would You help me walk through the test with joy?

Maintain a Fiery Hot Love Walk

God is love, so everything He thinks, says, and does is motivated by love. Because love is who God is, there is nothing He can do that contradicts love.

As ambassadors for Christ and ministers of reconciliation, we must cultivate a fiery hot love walk as a matter of importance. If we are not intentional about walking in love, we won't progress in this area. Praying in tongues helps us cultivate that love walk, burning away anything in us that hinders love.

Consider the words of Paul the apostle in First Corinthians 13:2, which cuts right to the heart of the matter: "And though I have the gift of prophecy, and understand all mysteries and all knowledge, and though I have all faith, so that I could remove mountains, but have not love, I am nothing."

And Jesus said, "By this all will know that you are My disciples, if you have love for one another" (John 13:35). Praying in tongues helps us to think loving thoughts, speak loving words, and take loving actions—all of which are central to displaying Christ's love to the world.

Scripture speaks incessantly about love. Paul expounded: "And now abide faith, hope, love, these three; but the greatest of these is love" (1 Cor. 13:13). First Corinthians 16:14 admonishes: "Let all that you do be done with love." And Ephesians 5:1-2 encourages, "Therefore be imitators of God as dear children. And walk in love, as Christ also has loved us and given Himself for us, an offering and a sacrifice to God for a sweet-smelling aroma." Praying in tongues powers up our love walk. We know what the love walk looks like:

> *Love suffers long and is kind; love does not envy; love does not parade itself, is not puffed up; does not behave rudely, does not seek its own, is not provoked, thinks no evil; does not rejoice in iniquity, but rejoices in the truth; bears all things, believes all things, hopes all things, endures all things. Love never fails. But whether there are prophecies, they will fail; whether there are tongues, they will cease; whether there is knowledge, it will vanish away* (1 Corinthians 13:4-8).

In my book *The Making of a Prophet*, I wrote, "Love will also safeguard your calling. Think about it. If you are walking in love, you are going to be obedient. If you are walking in love, you aren't going to merchandise God's people. If you are walking in love, you are going to be humble. If you are walking in love you are going to be gentle. The fruit of the Spirit is going to manifest in your life alongside the spiritual gifts."

Our love walk is central to our identity in Christ. We love Him because He first loved us, then we're able to love ourselves as we are while we grow—and love others as they are while they grow. None of us are perfect, but praying in tongues is one means by which God perfects us in love.

Prayer

Father, in the name of Jesus, I want to walk in love even with people who do not walk in love with me. Would You help me cultivate a fiery hot love walk as I pray in tongues?

Survive the Sifting

S atan wants to overthrow your faith. He wants to shake the faith right out of you.

Job was sifted. Peter was sifted. Praying in tongues helps you survive the sifting. Let's look at this concept in Scripture.

In Luke 22:31, Jesus told Peter clearly, "Simon, Simon! Indeed, Satan has asked for you, that he may sift you as wheat." *Sift* in this verse comes from the Greek word *siniazo*. Figuratively, it means "by inward agitation to try one's faith to the verge of overthrow." That's intense. To sift also means to sort through and remove what is not valuable from what is valuable. Praying in tongues helps you make it through the sifting.

The NET Bible translates Luke 22:31 this way: "Simon, Simon, pay attention! Satan has demanded to have you all, to sift you like wheat." See, it wasn't just Peter satan wanted to sift. It was all the disciples. Remember how they all scattered at the Garden of Gethsemane when Judas betrayed Jesus with a kiss? At the foot of the cross, as Jesus was hanging there naked, only John and the three Marys were present. Praying in tongues helps you make it through the sifting.

In the last days, Jesus said many will be offended. Many will walk away from Him. There is a sifting coming. It's called the Great Falling Away. Second Thessalonians 2:1-3 describes this time:

Now, brethren, concerning the coming of our Lord Jesus Christ and our gathering together to Him, we ask you, not to be soon shaken in mind or troubled, either by spirit or by word or by letter, as if from us, as though the day of Christ had come. Let no one deceive you by any means; for that Day will not come unless the falling away comes first, and the man of sin is revealed, the son of perdition.

But there's another kind of sifting. In Judges 7, Gideon's army was sifted before Israel battled the Midianites. In the first sifting, twenty-two thousand people were relieved of their assignment in the battle as fear disqualified them (see Judg. 7:3). That left ten thousand, but it was still too many. God instructed Gideon to tell the soldiers to drink from the water.

And the Lord said to Gideon, "Everyone who laps from the water with his tongue, as a dog laps, you shall set apart by himself; likewise everyone who gets down on his knees to drink." And the number of those who lapped, putting their hand to their mouth, was three hundred men; but all the rest of the people got down on their knees to drink water. Then the Lord said to Gideon, "By the three hundred men who lapped I will save you, and deliver the Midianites into your hand. Let all the other people go, every man to his place" (Judges 7:5-7).

I don't want to get swept up in the Great Falling Away. I want to be counted worthy in the battle. I don't want to watch from the sidelines. Praying in tongues helps you survive the sifting of your faith.

Prayer

Father, in the name of Jesus, help me survive the sifting as the enemy comes to test my mettle. As I pray in tongues, remove the fear and break deception off my mind so I can stand and withstand.

Tapping into Divine Endurance

Endurance is the ability to withstand hardship or adversity. It's the ability to sustain a prolonged stressful effort or activity. We need endurance from enemy temptations, endurance in trials, endurance in spiritual warfare, endurance to do the will of God, and more. Praying in tongues helps you endure the rigors of this world.

The writer of Hebrews backs me up: "For you have need of endurance, so that after you have done the will of God, you may receive the promise" (Heb. 10:36). Sometimes God calls us to do difficult things, and the enemy resists us as we seek to do the will of God. Praying in tongues helps us endure because we're activating the strength of the Spirit of God.

The writer of Hebrews also reminds: "Therefore we also, since we are surrounded by so great a cloud of witnesses, let us lay aside every weight, and the sin which so easily ensnares us, and let us run with endurance the race that is set before us, looking unto Jesus" (Heb. 12:1-2). If Jesus endured His cross, and He did, you can also endure your cross. Praying in tongues helps you endure your cross.

Paul offers some awesome revelation in Romans 15:5: "May the God of endurance and encouragement grant you to live in such harmony with one another, in accord with Christ Jesus" (ESV). Catch that. God is a God of endurance—and you were created in His image. When you pray in tongues, you are tapping into God's own strength to endure.

Listen, in the end times we're going to need endurance. And there are rewards associated with endurance. Revelation 3:10 speaks these words to the church at Philadelphia, but they can encourage us today: "Because you have kept my word about patient endurance, I will keep you from the hour of trial that is coming on the whole world, to try those who dwell on the earth" (ESV). Praying in tongues helps give us endurance to keep His Word.

Over and over again, we're called to endure. Revelation 13:10 tells us, "Here is a call for the endurance and faith of the saints" (ESV). And Revelation 14:12 echoes, "Here is a call for the endurance of the saints, those who keep the commandments of God and their faith in Jesus" (ESV). Jesus also said in Matthew 10:22, "And you will be hated by all for my name's sake. But the one who endures to the end will be saved" (ESV). Praying in tongues will help you endure to the end.

Finally, consider Second Timothy 2:10-12: "Therefore I endure all things for the sake of the elect, that they also may obtain the salvation which is in Christ Jesus with eternal glory. This is a faithful saying: For if we died with Him, we shall also live with Him. If we endure, we shall also reign with Him. If we deny Him, He also will deny us." When we endure to the end, we will reign with Him. Keep praying in tongues!

Prayer

Father, in the name of Jesus, I need endurance. As I pray in tongues, help me to tap into Your endurance, which never fails or falters. Make me strong in the Lord to stand and withstand anything that comes my way.

Anticipate the Blindside

We are not supposed to be blindsided by the enemy. We are supposed to hear the roar of the lion and the hiss of the snake. We are supposed to discern the weapon forming against us so we can dismantle it before it has a chance to prosper. Praying in tongues can help you anticipate and avoid the blindside.

What do I mean by "blindside"? *Merriam-Webster*'s dictionary defines *blindside* as, "to hit unexpectedly from or as if from the blind side" and "to surprise unpleasantly." *Blindside* also means, "the side away from which one is looking."

Praying in tongues helps you eliminate your blind side. Remember, First Peter 5:8 says, "Be sober, be vigilant; because your adversary the devil walks about like a roaring lion, seeking whom he may devour." The Holy Spirit can make you sensitive to see something you couldn't see. Praying in tongues helps you stay vigilant, alertly watchful to avoid danger and enemy attacks.

The New Living Translation of this verse puts it this way: "Stay alert! Watch out for your great enemy, the devil. He prowls around like a roaring lion, looking for someone to devour." Praying in tongues helps you stay alert and watch out for your great enemy so he can't sneak up on you. You will sniff him out in the spirit from miles away.

The New American Standard Bible translates First Peter 5:8 like this: "Be of sober spirit, be on the alert. Your adversary, the devil, prowls around like a roaring lion, seeking someone to devour." Praying in tongues helps you keep a sober spirit and mind, which is commanded in several Scriptures.

Paul tells us in First Thessalonians 5:6 to be awake and sober, which means not only refraining from drunkenness but also having a thoughtful, serious demeanor. Paul also tells his spiritual sons Timothy and Titus to be sober-minded (see 1 Tim. 3:2; Titus 2:2). And Peter tells us to be sober-minded for the sake of our prayers (see 1 Pet. 4:7). Praying in tongues helps us fulfill this command.

The Amplified Classic version expounds on First Peter 5:8: "Be well balanced (temperate, sober of mind), be vigilant and cautious at all times; for that enemy of yours, the devil, roams around like a lion roaring [in fierce hunger], seeking someone to seize upon and devour." Your enemy is hungry. He's itching to steal, kill, and destroy. He knows if you discern his entrance into your garden, you will crush his head. That's why he works to orchestrate a blindside attack.

In fact, The Contemporary English Version of this scripture puts it plainly: "Be on your guard and stay awake. Your enemy, the devil, is like a roaring lion, sneaking around to find someone to attack." Praying in tongues can cut down on enemy attacks because it helps you to stay on your guard. An enemy exposed is an enemy defeated.

Prayer

Father, in the name of Jesus, would You help me stay sober-minded and alert? As I pray in tongues over the warfare I feel looming, would You expose the enemy of my soul so I can resist him and overtake him?

Positioned for Proper Pruning

P runing is part of our Christian walk. You will be pruned if you do and pruned if you don't. In other words, pruning is unavoidable, but praying in tongues helps position us for proper pruning. We don't want to behave like the toddler who doesn't want a haircut.

John 15:1-8 talks about Jesus as the vine and the Father as the vine dresser. He said:

> *I am the true vine, and My Father is the vinedresser. Every branch in Me that bears no fruit, He takes away. And every branch that bears fruit, He prunes, that it may bear more fruit. You are already clean through the word which I have spoken to you. Remain in Me, as I also remain in you. As the branch cannot bear fruit by itself, unless it remains in the vine, neither can you, unless you remain in Me.*
>
> *I am the vine, you are the branches. He who remains in Me, and I in him, bears much fruit. For without Me you can do nothing. If a man does not remain in Me, he is thrown out as a branch and withers. And they gather them and throw them into the fire, and they are burned. If you remain in Me, and My words remain in you, you will ask whatever you desire, and it shall be done for you. My Father is glorified by this, that you bear much fruit; so you will be My disciples* (MEV).

The Greek word for *prune* in these verses is *kathario*. According to *The KJV New Testament Greek Lexicon*, it means "to cleanse, of filth impurity, etc." *Merriam-Webster*'s dictionary defines *prune* as "to reduce especially by eliminating superfluous matter" and "to cut off or cut back parts of for better shape or more fruitful growth." Praying in tongues positions you for the pruning, to walk through it gracefully.

At times, we get too comfortable with the status quo. We get stuck in our comfort zone. When that happens, God may start pruning away the things you won't willingly give Him. In other words, He is often trying to get us to a new glory, a new promotion, a new fill-in-the-blank—but we won't let go of the old. Therefore, in His kindness, He prunes away the things that hinder growth. We don't like it. It doesn't feel good. But it's necessary.

This spiritual principle is also found in Leviticus 25:3-4:

> *Six years you shall sow your field, and six years you shall prune your vineyard, and gather its fruit; but in the seventh year there shall be a sabbath of solemn rest for the land, a sabbath to the Lord. You shall neither sow your field nor prune your vineyard.*

Sometimes, after a pruning we see no growth for a while. We feel stuck. We don't know what's going on. It's a wilderness, of sorts. Praying in tongues helps you work through the pruning seasons with confidence in God's hand on your life.

Prayer

Father, in the name of Jesus, I don't like the pruning but I agree that it's necessary. As I pray in tongues, would You help me discern Your pruning shears at work in my life and walk in grace and trust with Your Spirit through the process?

Move in the Opposite Spirit

If you've been maligned, talked about, persecuted, betrayed, or otherwise treated poorly, you have two choices: you can return evil for evil or return good for evil. You can choose to move in the opposite spirit.

Praying in tongues helps you move in the opposite direction of demons and even your flesh. You can't take authority over the devil when you are acting like the devil. Praying in tongues helps you to submit yourself to God so you can resist the devil that's working through a person to hurt you.

Once I was in a foreign nation. They didn't like Christians, and they were hazing me. They gave me food with metal shards in it, took me on a nauseating boat ride in a dirty, choppy ocean, and left me stranded in various venues wondering if anyone would show up. I was about to get on a plane and go home when the Holy Spirit told me, "If a man compels you to walk a mile, walk two" (see Matt. 5:41). I had to pray in tongues to obey that Scripture as the hazing continued.

Jesus told us in the Sermon on the Mount to bless those who persecute us. That is one way to move in the opposite spirit, as is walking the extra mile, turning the other cheek, and giving up your coat if they ask for your shirt. Indeed, Jesus' teaching was a far cry from the world's ways—or even the Law's ways that commanded an eye for an eye and a tooth for a tooth. Praying in tongues helps you find the strength to move in the opposite spirit rather than lashing out.

See, the carnal mind wants to strike back twice as hard, file a countersuit, tell everyone who will listen what they did to you, make them pay. To stand there and take it, to give away even more than what someone is trying to force from your hands, to pray a blessing on the ones who are cursing you—that, my friends, is called moving in the opposite spirit, and there's a reward in it.

When you move in the opposite spirit, you avoid the bondage that the one who strikes you, sues you, takes advantage of you, gives you a hard time, or mistreats you in any way is living in. You walk free—you walk in power. And your response might even set them free, too. We overcome evil with good. Praying in the spirit helps you move in the opposite spirit.

Remember this: you can't try to move in the opposite spirit. Not really. Apart from Christ, you can do nothing, but all things are possible in His strength. When we move in the opposite spirit of the ones who come against us, we are moving in the Holy Spirit. When we pray in tongues with a mind to obey the Sermon on the Mount instructions, it helps us act like Christ in the face of accusers and abusers.

Prayer

Father, in the name of Jesus, I don't like to be lied to, harmed, and hazed, but I want to obey Your Word. As I pray in tongues, would You help me to move in the opposite spirit so I can maintain my authority in Christ?

Handle Persecution Like a Pro

Persecution is a reality for every single solitary Christian. While we are not likely to be beheaded for refusing to denounce Jesus, there are more subtle forms of persecution we'll all face at one point or another. Praying in tongues helps us handle persecution like a pro.

Paul verifies the unfortunate reality of the persecuted Christian in Second Timothy 3:12: "Yes, and all who desire to live godly in Christ Jesus will suffer persecution." It's not a matter of if, but when you will face persecution. How you handle persecution is important. Praying in tongues helps you handle persecution with class.

Persecution—which means to harass or punish in a way that seeks to cause someone personal injury and suffering—occurs for many reasons. For example, in the Parable of the Sower, Jesus said, "Afterward, when tribulation or persecution arises for the word's sake, immediately they stumble" (Mark 4:17).

Some of your persecution comes for the Word's sake. Many times, after the Lord gives you a revelation from the Word, the enemy will come to test you on it. Praying in tongues helps you resist stumbling in the midst of that persecution. Praying in tongues is like watering the seed of the word the Lord plants in your heart.

David understood persecution better than most of us ever will. In Psalm 143:3-8, he wrote:

For the enemy has persecuted my soul; he has crushed my life to the ground; he has made me dwell in darkness, like those who have long been dead. Therefore my spirit is overwhelmed within me; my heart within me is distressed.

I remember the days of old; I meditate on all Your works; I muse on the work of Your hands. I spread out my hands to You; my soul longs for You like a thirsty land. Selah

Answer me speedily, O Lord; my spirit fails! Do not hide Your face from me, lest I be like those who go down into the pit. Cause me to hear Your lovingkindness in the morning, for in You do I trust; cause me to know the way in which I should walk, for I lift up my soul to You.

Maybe you can relate to David's plight. When you feel like this, pray in tongues because your soul may be too distraught to pray in your native language. Worship in tongues and remember what Peter said: "If you are reproached for the name of Christ, blessed are you, for the Spirit of glory and of God rests upon you" (1 Pet. 4:14). When you pray in tongues during persecution, instead of feeling sorry for yourself you invite the Spirit and glory of God to rest on you in a tangible way.

Remember this. Jesus said in Matthew 5:44, "But I say to you, love your enemies, bless those who curse you, do good to those who hate you, and pray for those who spitefully use you and persecute you." Why not pray for them in tongues? If you can't seem to find it in you to pray for them in English, pray for them in tongues to obey this command and protect your heart from unforgiveness.

Prayer

Father, in the name of Jesus, I know there's no escaping persecution, as much as I might try. As I pray in tongues, would You strengthen me to handle persecution like Jesus, turning the other cheek and walking the extra mile?

BENEFIT 70

Mega Grace to Forgive

We have the opportunity to get offended many times a week—or even several times a day depending on our relational context. Think about it for a minute. Just driving down the road in bad traffic can send some people into a rage. Other people have toxic bosses, abusive pastors, or even angry spouses.

When someone hurts or offends us, we don't usually feel like forgiving. Quite the opposite, in fact, our emotions rise up and if we are not careful we will act out and even lash out. Many people tell me in pastoral counseling, "I can't forgive. You don't understand. I tried and I can't!"

The reality is, you can forgive but in the moment you don't want to. You want to hold a grudge. I know it seems impossible through the eyes of pain, but forgiveness is a force of our will. We can choose to forgive. Praying in tongues makes our heart pliable and helps release the grace of forgivingness. Pray in tongues until you feel the grace to say the words, "I forgive you."

Jesus said in Mark 11:25, "And whenever you stand praying, forgive, if you have anything against anyone, so that your Father also who is in heaven may forgive you your trespasses" (ESV). God won't hear your prayers when you are in unforgiveness. It's a serious issue. What's more, unforgiveness invites tormenting spirits into your life (see Matt. 18:34). Praying in tongues helps you tap into mega grace to forgive.

As part of the famed Lord's Prayer, Jesus said, "And forgive us our debts, as we forgive our debtors. And do not lead us into temptation, but deliver us from the evil one. For Yours is the kingdom and the power and the glory forever. Amen" (Matt. 6:11-13). Then, He immediately said in verse 14: "For if you forgive men their trespasses, your heavenly Father will also forgive you."

This is a serious issue that we can't afford to ignore. Ask yourself this question: What if the Lord forgave you in the same proportion that you forgave the people who hurt you? What if God forgave you halfway or held a grudge? Would you feel comfortable with that? If not, pray in tongues until you can bring yourself to forgive.

Jesus said in Matthew 5:44, "But I say to you, love your enemies, bless those who curse you, do good to those who hate you, and pray for those who spitefully use you and persecute you." Paul stressed, "And be kind to one another, tenderhearted, forgiving one another, even as God in Christ forgave you" (Eph. 4:32). And again, "Bearing with one another, and forgiving one another, if anyone has a complaint against another; even as Christ forgave you, so you also must do" (Col. 3:13). This is the foundation of Christianity, folks.

Remember Peter and John and their somewhat competitive relationship? "Then Peter came to Him and said, 'Lord, how often shall my brother sin against me, and I forgive him? Up to seven times?' Jesus said to him, 'I do not say to you, up to seven times, but up to seventy times seven'" (Matt. 18:21-22).

If you are not sure if you have forgiveness, praying in tongues can also enlighten your heart to the bitterness and resentment. Pray in tongues with a mind toward forgiveness.

Prayer

Father, in the name of Jesus, I choose by force of my will to forgive. As I pray in tongues would You show me any unforgiveness in the deep recesses of my soul? Would You help me tap into the grace of forgiveness so I can walk in freedom?

Avoid the Enemy's Snares

The enemy lays snares in our path, looking to trap us and isolate us so he can execute his ministry of stealing, killing, and destroying (see John 10:10). His snares are disguised and invisible to the naked eye, but they can be discerned in the spirit.

Remember, you can't take everything at face value. Animals don't fall into snares on purpose. They either don't see it or they take the bait and find themselves hoodwinked.

Job 18:8-10 reveals the enemy's snare strategy: "For he is cast into a net by his own feet, and he walks into a snare. The net takes him by the heel, and a snare lays hold of him. A noose is hidden for him on the ground, and a trap for him in the road." Notice how the enemy's target walked right into the snare.

What is a snare? According to *Merriam-Webster's* dictionary, a snare is something by which one is entangled, involved in difficulties, or impeded or something deceptively attractive. A snare could be the enemy's bait, lure, decoy, or trick to put you in bondage.

Praying in tongues helps you avoid the snare. I believe I've avoided many snares through praying in tongues, and sometimes I never even knew the snares were there until a later point in time. I've avoided snares set by false prophets, snares set by Jezebelic believers, snares set by tempting devils, and more.

Psalm 91:3 tells us, "Surely He shall deliver you from the snare of the fowler and from the perilous pestilence." *Snare* also means "to capture by or as if by use of a snare."

Wrong relationships can be snares. I've avoided snares in getting involved with the wrong people through a "knowing" that came to my heart after praying in tongues. Everything looked well and fine on the outside, but the Holy Spirit saw what was going on in the person's heart and warned me so I could disconnect quickly.

Beyond casual relationships, a snare could be a covenant with the wrong person, such as a business partner or a marriage. Exodus 34:12, "Take care, lest you make a covenant with the inhabitants of the land to which you go, lest it become a snare in your midst" (ESV). Pray in tongues before you enter into a covenant. It can save you a lot of trouble.

A snare could be offense. A snare could be the love of money, which is a root of all evil. First Timothy 6:9 warns, "But those who desire to be rich fall into temptation and a snare, and into many foolish and harmful lusts which drown men in destruction and perdition."

I've avoided snares of making big purchases that would have wasted my money after praying in tongues over an issue. Indeed, I've avoided all kinds of snares by praying in tongues and receiving the revelation I needed to avoid the trap. Again, you don't always see what the Lord is doing until later on.

Prayer

Father, in the name of Jesus, help me see the enemy's snare so I can avoid it. As I pray in tongues, would You show me the snares of the fowlers? Would You lead me around and away from the enemy's snares?

Walk in the Spirit of Counsel

I love the spirit of counsel. It's one of the seven spirits of God mentioned in Isaiah 11:2. Counsel is one of the seven attributes of the Holy Spirit. When you need to stand in that role of counselor, the Holy Spirit can counsel through you when you give yourself over to praying in tongues.

The word *counsel* in Isaiah 11:2 comes from the Hebrew word *etsah*, which means "counsel, advice, purpose," according to *The KJV Old Testament Hebrew Lexicon*. One translation calls it a spirit of advice. *Merriam-Webster*'s dictionary defines *counsel* as "advice given especially as a result of consultation, a policy or plan of action or behavior, guarded thoughts or intentions." Praying in tongues helps you tap into the spirit of counsel so you can give wise advice.

Of course, Jesus is called Wonderful Counselor in Isaiah 9:6. And the Holy Spirit is referred to as our Counselor in many translations of the Bible. A counselor is someone who offers guidance. The Holy Spirit, our Counselor, leads us and guides us into all truth. When the spirit of counsel comes up on us, we can share the Holy Spirit's divine instruction. Praying in tongues invites the spirit of counsel.

Although the spirit of counsel can inform you—the Holy Spirit can counsel you directly—generally speaking the spirit of counsel is intended for you to minister to others. Proverbs 27:9 tells us, "A man's counsel is sweet to his friend" (NASB95). How many of you know that counsel is only sweet if it is inspired by our Wonderful Counselor?

Many times I've received counsel that was not godly and the end result was bitter. I was led in the absolute wrong direction. The person was not operating out of a spirit of counsel but their own opinion or their own wisdom—or even their own desire. If you are going to take responsibility for guiding someone's life, you should be praying in tongues with a mind to tap into the spirit of counsel. It's the responsible thing to do.

The spirit of counsel is especially helpful for those who do counseling and deliverance, but certainly every believer needs to counsel others from time to time. I remember a difficult deliverance session where I hit a wall. Suddenly, without even knowing it, the spirit of counsel came upon me and I had wisdom from heaven to help a couple work through issues that set them both free.

When I am dealing with a difficult situation, I want someone with the spirit of counsel on them like Ahithophel. We read about him in Second Samuel 16:23, "Now the advice of Ahithophel, which he gave in those days, was as if one had inquired at the oracle of God. So was all the advice of Ahithophel both with David and with Absalom."

We also see the spirit of counsel on Jethro, Moses' father-in-law: "Listen now to my voice; I will give you counsel, and God will be with you: Stand before God for the people, so that you may bring the difficulties to God" (Exod. 18:19). The spirit of counsel is available to you to serve others. Praying in tongues helps you tap into it.

Prayer

Father, in the name of Jesus, thank You that the Wonderful Counselor lives on the inside of me and His counsel is available to me. When I pray in tongues, would You help me tap into the spirit of counsel to give Your people wise advice?

Unlock the Spirit of Might

God's Word tells us to be strong in the Lord and the power of His might (see Eph. 6:10). We're not supposed to fight the enemy in our own strength, but in His strength, with His Word, in His name, and by His blood.

Thankfully, Isaiah 11:2 speaks of the spirit of might, which is one of the seven spirits of God, or one of the seven attributes of the Holy Spirit. Praying in tongues can help you tap into the spirit of might so that you have the strength, power, and fortitude to execute God's plan despite enemy interference.

Strong's Concordance translates the Hebrew word for *might*, which is *geburah*, as "force, mastery, might, mighty act, power, power, strength"—and we can tap into this spirit of might by praying in tongues.

The Berean Study Bible calls it the spirit of strength. The International Standard Version calls it the spirit of power. The NET Bible says "a Spirit that provides the ability to execute plans." Another translation calls it a spirit of fortitude. Whatever you call it, I want it.

In Second Chronicles 27:6, we read about a man named Jotham who was king of Judah: "So Jotham became mighty, because he ordered his ways before the Lord his God" (ESV). Jotham was unable to wage war against the Ammonites and defeat them in his own strength. But when he was weak, the Lord was strong. He did it through the spirit of might.

When you pray in tongues, you are ordering your ways before the Lord your God, and you are positioning yourself for the spirit of might to rest on you. Your God is mighty!

Zephaniah 3:17 reminds us: "The Lord your God in your midst, the Mighty One, will save; He will rejoice over you with gladness, He will quiet you with His love, He will rejoice over you with singing." And Deuteronomy 10:17 assures us, "For the Lord your God is God of gods and Lord of lords, the great God, mighty and awesome, who shows no partiality nor takes a bribe."

When you pray in tongues, you may be beckoning the Mighty One to show up and save you from peril. Psalm 66:7 makes it plain: "He rules by His might forever; His eyes keep watch on the nations; the rebellious shall not exalt themselves! Selah" (NASB). Remember, God is not just mighty, He's almighty! Jesus shows forth His might in Revelation 1:8, "'I am the Alpha and the Omega, the Beginning and the End,' says the Lord, 'who is and who was and who is to come, the Almighty.'"

The spirit of might will enable you to experience what Paul described in First Corinthians as making you immovable. "Therefore, my beloved brothers, be steadfast, immovable, always abounding in the work of the Lord, knowing that in the Lord your labor is not in vain" (1 Cor. 15:58 ESV). Praying in tongues can release the spirit of might over you!

Prayer

Father, in the name of Jesus, I know I can't resist the enemy or overcome him in my own strength. But when I am weak You are strong. As I pray in tongues, would You let the spirit of might rest upon me?

Walk in the Spirit of the Fear of the Lord

What the church—and the world—needs now is the spirt of the fear of the Lord. Jesus, our Savior and Lord, is worthy of our reverence. What's more, there are biblical benefits to embracing the spirit of the fear of the Lord.

Isaiah 11:2 speaks of the spirit of the fear of the Lord. Praying in tongues helps you cultivate this heart posture. Praying in tongues helps you walk in the fear of the Lord consistently as a lifestyle.

Before I move on, let's define the fear of the Lord by looking at some Greek and Hebrew words. One definition of the Hebrew word *yare* means "to fear, to respect, to reverence."

The Greek word *phobos* can be translated "reverential fear." *Vine's Complete Expository Dictionary* defines it as "not a mere 'fear' of His power and righteous retribution, but a wholesome dread of displeasing Him." That's intense!

Jesus said in Matthew 10:28, "And do not fear those who kill the body but cannot kill the soul. But rather fear Him who is able to destroy both soul and body in hell."

Praying in tongues helps you walk in the fear of the Lord, but how do we walk in it? For starters, "The fear of the Lord is to hate evil" (Prov. 8:13). And the benefits are many. For example, "The fear of the Lord is the beginning of wisdom" (Prov. 9:10). What's more, "The fear of the Lord is the beginning of knowledge" (Prov. 1:7).

Do you want to know God's secrets? Pray in tongues. Psalm 25:14 tells us, "The secret of the Lord is with those who fear Him." Can you see how these benefits are directly connected to walking in a spirit of the fear of the Lord? But wait, that's not all.

How many of you want provision? Pray in tongues for the spirit of the fear of the Lord to rest upon you. "There is no want to those who fear Him" (Ps. 34:9). Want more? Proverbs 14:27 tells us, "The fear of the Lord is a fountain of life." And Proverbs 22:4 assures, "By humility and the fear of the Lord are riches and honor and life."

Do you want mercy for your generations? Walk in the fear of the Lord. Pray in tongues as Luke 1:50 promises: "And His mercy is on those who fear Him from generation to generation." And Proverbs 14:26: "In the fear of the Lord there is strong confidence, and His children will have a place of refuge."

If there is one thing I have going for me, I walk in a fear of the Lord most of the time. If you want to cultivate or welcome the spirit of the fear of the Lord in your life, praying in tongues is one way to do that.

The preacher said in Ecclesiastes 12:13, "Let us hear the conclusion of the whole matter: Fear God and keep His commandments, for this is man's all." Amen.

Prayer

Father, in the name of Jesus, I want to walk in the fear of the Lord consistently. As I pray in tongues, would You release the spirit of the fear of the Lord over my life so I can honor You in all my ways?

Release Prayers at the Speed of Light

As the legend has it, comic book favorite Superman traveled faster than the speed of light. Of course, that's fiction, but our supernatural prayers in tongues could outpace Superman on his best day.

Let's dig into this. The speed of sound and the speed of light are different. According to Live Science, "On Earth, the speed of sound at sea level—assuming an air temperature of 59 degrees Fahrenheit (15 degrees Celsius)—is 761.2 mph (1,225 km/h)." According to Space .com, the speed of light in a vacuum is 186,282 miles per second (299,792 kilometers per second), and in theory nothing can travel faster than light. In miles per hour, light speed is, well, a lot—about 670,616,629 miles per hour. If you could travel at the speed of light, you could go around the Earth 7.5 times in one second.

That's a lot of math. But the bottom line, is when you pray in tongues—although you are uttering a sound—the prayers are actually traveling faster than the speed of light. You could, then, call them superhero prayers. But then again, it's even faster. When you pray in tongues, you are releasing super conqueror petitions (see Rom. 8:37).

We see evidence of how fast our prayers travel throughout the pages of Scripture. For example, Isaiah 65:24 reads, "It shall come to pass that before they call, I will answer; and while they are still speaking, I will hear." Before we finish praying a complete sentence in tongues, God is already hearing and answering.

The New Living Translation of that verse reads, "I will answer them before they even call to me. While they are still talking about their needs, I will go ahead and answer their prayers!" And The Voice translation says, "I'll anticipate their prayers and respond before they know it; even as they speak, I will hear." There's no time lag on prayer.

Second Kings 20 tells the story of a king named Hezekiah who was deathly ill. Isaiah the prophet went to him and told him to get his house in order because he was going to die. The king turned his face to the wall and prayed for the Lord to spare him and wept bitterly.

> *And it happened, before Isaiah had gone out into the middle court, that the word of the Lord came to him, saying, "Return and tell Hezekiah the leader of My people, 'Thus says the Lord, the God of David your father: "I have heard your prayer, I have seen your tears; surely I will heal you. On the third day you shall go up to the house of the Lord. And I will add to your days fifteen years. I will deliver you and this city from the hand of the king of Assyria; and I will defend this city for My own sake, and for the sake of My servant David"'" (2 Kings 20:4-6).*

Hezekiah went on to live his life. A quick prayer caused God to stop the prophet dead in his tracks to give him a new word that overruled the first word. God anticipates our prayers. When we pray in tongues, we're praying at breakneck speed.

Prayer

Father, thank You that before I ever open my mouth to release my tongues You know what I am going to pray and are ready to take action on my behalf. As I pray in tongues, help me recognize Your faster-than-light answers on my behalf so I can praise You all the more.

Tap into the Spirit of Knowledge

It's been said that knowledge is power. Certainly God's knowledge empowers us, liberates us, and inspires us. Praying in tongues helps us tap into the spirit of knowledge, which is one of the seven spirits of God we find listed in Isaiah 11:2.

You can gain knowledge through reading or through experience. You can gain knowledge through awareness and reasoning. But the spirit of knowledge takes your knowing to a whole new level. The Hebrew word for *knowledge* in Isaiah 11:2 includes knowledge, perception, skill, discernment, understanding, and wisdom. That's an attractive package deal.

The spirit of knowledge is not book knowledge; this is a more intimate understanding of who the Lord is and His ways. With this kind of knowledge, the enemy of your soul can't stop you. You can tap into that spirt of knowledge by praying in tongues.

Consider Psalm 94:10: "He who instructs the nations, shall He not correct, He who teaches man knowledge?" When you pray in tongues, the Holy Spirit is teaching you knowledge of God. It's the knowledge of the holy.

A.W. Tozer wrote a book called *The Knowledge of the Holy*. In it, he wrote, "What comes to our minds when we think about God is the most important thing about us." The more we know God, the more we will know what to do or how to respond in any given situation.

Noteworthy is the prophecy from Hosea: "My people are destroyed for lack of knowledge" (Hos. 4:6). It's not book knowledge the Israelites were lacking. They were aware of the commandments. It was a knowledge of the Lord in a more intimate way. Praying in tongues helps you tap into that knowledge of the Lord.

In Second Peter 3:18, Peter prayed, "But grow in the grace and knowledge of our Lord and Savior Jesus Christ. To Him be the glory both now and forever. Amen." You can grow in the knowledge of our Lord by praying in tongues.

In Colossians 1:9, Paul the apostle prayed that the members of the church at Corinth would be filled with the spirit of knowledge: "For this reason we also, since the day we heard it, do not cease to pray for you, and to ask that you may be filled with the knowledge of His will in all wisdom and spiritual understanding." Praying in tongues helps us access what is really already in us and grow in knowledge according to Second Peter 1:5: "But also for this very reason, giving all diligence, add to your faith virtue, to virtue knowledge."

Most of all, we need to know the love of Christ. Ephesians 3:19 helps us understand that we need to go beyond head knowledge to heart knowledge.

> *[That you may really come] to know [practically, through experience for yourselves] the love of Christ, which far surpasses mere knowledge [without experience]; that you may be filled [through all your being] unto all the fullness of God [may have the richest measure of the divine Presence, and become a body wholly filled and flooded with God Himself]!* (AMPC)

Prayer

Father, in the name of Jesus, I want to pursue the knowledge of You, Your thoughts, and Your ways. As I pray in tongues, would You give me access to the spirit of knowledge so I can receive knowledge, perception, skill, discernment, understanding, and wisdom about Your generous Spirit?

Prophesy Your Future

Always remember this: You are your own best prophet. And get this: When you are praying in tongues you may be unknowingly prophesying your future. See, the Holy Spirit knows all things, including every step on the way to your destiny. The Holy Spirit is the spirit of prophecy, and He can testify through you what Jesus wants to do in your life as you pray in tongues.

Think about it for a minute. What you speak over your life is perhaps more important than what anyone else speaks—except God. When you yield your tongue to the Holy Spirit's utterance, you are letting Him speak the Father's will over your life.

Our own tongues can derail God's plans for our lives in any season. That's why when Zechariah rejected Gabriel's prophecy about his wife Elizabeth bearing a son, the messenger angel muted him until John the Baptist was born. Zechariah was operating in unbelief and the angel did not want him disagreeing with God's plan for his family.

God is not going to mute your mouth for a season if you speak in unbelief. We have free rein to yield our tongue to the devil. We have a free will to prophesy doom and gloom over our lives by coming into agreement verbally with the wicked one's lies. Alternatively, we can yield our tongues to the Holy Spirit as we pray and believe that His prophetic words over our life will come to pass.

Our tongues hold great power. Proverbs 18:21 tells us, "Death and life are in the power of the tongue, and they who indulge in it shall eat the fruit of it [for death or life]" (AMPC). When you speak in tongues, you are speaking words of life over your situations, circumstances—and even your destiny. You may be prophesying into your future life—the future and the hope God has promised His children (see Jer. 29:11).

There have been times when I started praying in tongues and I literally felt a shift in my heart, a shift in my mind, and a shift in my circumstances—even if it wasn't yet visible. Sometimes, the Holy Spirit will show me what He is prophesying over my life so I can come into agreement with my natural mind.

If you sense the prophetic spirit brooding over you as you release your tongues, take Paul's advice in First Corinthians 14:13: "Therefore let him who speaks in a tongue pray that he may interpret." Pray for the interpretation, then stay silent and wait on Him to reveal His prophetic words. It's up to Him whether He shows you. Sometimes if we knew what He was prophesying we would be tempted to get ahead of Him.

Now, you can prophesy over yourself in your native language. I have prophesied over myself before. But you can't choose to prophesy over yourself. The Holy Spirit is the source of prophecy, as He shares the testimony of Jesus (see Rev. 19:10). He has to give you the words.

Proverbs 16:24 offers: "Kind words are like honey—sweet to the soul and healthy for the body" (NLT). When the Holy Spirit prophesies over you, He's prophesying kind words. You don't have to worry about what you say when you pray in tongues.

Prayer

Father, in the name of Jesus, as I yield my tongue to Your words of life would You prophesy Your will over my life? Would You give me a glimpse into my future and hope in Christ as I wait in Your presence for the interpretation?

BENEFIT 78

Wage War
with Prophetic Words

Paul the apostle prayed in tongues more than anyone—and I'd like to believe he warred in tongues more than anyone as well. Remember, Paul had prophecies from Ananias over his life. Ananias was the prophet God chose to lay hands on Paul after he was blinded on the road to Damascus on his church-persecuting mission.

The Lord told the prophet, "Go, for he is a chosen vessel of Mine to bear My name before Gentiles, kings, and the children of Israel. For I will show him how many things he must suffer for My name's sake" (Acts 9:15-16). Paul received prophetic instruction, and I believe the apostle had to keep those words in mind—and even war with them. You can war with the prophecies God, or prophets, speak over your life as you pray in tongues.

Paul shared this concept with his spiritual son Timothy in First Timothy 1:18, "This command I commit to you, my son Timothy, according to the prophecies that were previously given to you, that by them you might fight a good fight" (MEV). Note that this was not a suggestion but a command.

The Amplified Classic translation of that verse exhorts us to be "inspired and aided" by the prophetic words so that "you may wage the good warfare." The New Living Translation tells us that the prophetic words "help you fight well in the Lord's battles." And *The Message* tells us the prophecies should make you "fearless in your struggle, keeping a firm grip on your faith and on yourself. After all, this is a fight we're in."

The Holy Spirit is an expert warrior. He's never, not once in all of eternity past, lost a battle. He is as invested in seeing the prophetic words over life come to pass as you are. In fact, He may be even more invested in seeing the prophetic words over your life come to pass than you are. The reality is most personal prophecy is conditional. We have a part and God has a part, and the enemy resists us throughout the process.

We have to fight the good fight of faith (see 1 Tim. 6:12). We can fight that good fight of faith by decreeing, declaring, and re-prophesying the words over our life. But we can also fight the good fight of faith over those utterances by giving utterance to the Holy Spirit's voice as we pray in tongues.

Amos 3:3 asks a pointed question, "Can two walk together, unless they are agreed?" When we pray in tongues, we are submitting our will to His will as He prays the perfect prayer—and sometimes engages in the perfect warfare—on our behalf. We are coming into agreement with what He wants, even if we don't understand what we're praying.

You may notice sometimes your tongues sound different, perhaps aggressive or violent. Jesus told us, "And from the days of John the Baptist until now the kingdom of heaven suffers violence, and the violent take it by force" (Matt. 11:12). If your tongues sound forceful or violent, just flow with it. That may be the Holy Spirit waging war over the prophecies about your life.

Prayer

Father, in the name of Jesus, would You help me discern when You are on the war path against the enemy of the prophecies spoken over my life? Help me to yield my voice to Your utterance as You wage war against my spiritual enemies.

Bind and Loose

Jesus said in John 10:10, "The thief comes only in order to steal and kill and destroy. I came that they may have and enjoy life, and have it in abundance (to the full, till it overflows)" (AMPC).

God has a plan to loose joy, abundance, and overflow into your life. The enemy, alternatively, has a plan to bind you up. When you pray in tongues, you may be binding the enemy's plans and loosing God's best in your life.

Jesus gave us the keys to the Kingdom: "I will give you the keys of the kingdom of heaven, and whatever you bind on earth will be bound in heaven, and whatever you loose on earth will be loosed in heaven" (Matt. 16:19). Remember, when you release your tongues you are praying the perfect prayer. The good, perfect, and acceptable will of God is loosed over your life.

The Amplified Classic translation gives us more insight into how to use these keys successfully in spiritual warfare: "I will give you the keys of the kingdom of heaven; and whatever you bind (declare to be improper and unlawful) on earth must be what is already bound in heaven; and whatever you loose (declare lawful) on earth must be what is already loosed in heaven."

When you pray in tongues with a mind toward loosing God's will and binding the enemy's plans, you are essentially declaring the work of the devil improper and unlawful. You are appealing to God in the authority of Christ to put a cease-and-desist order on the enemy's operations against you. You are also declaring what God has deemed lawful for your life according to heaven's paradigm.

I love the New Living Translation of this verse with its forceful language: "And I will give you the keys of the Kingdom of Heaven. Whatever you forbid on earth will be forbidden in heaven, and whatever you permit on earth will be permitted in heaven."

When you pray in tongues with a mind toward shutting down the enemy's plans, the Holy Spirit is praying with you to enforce God's rule of law in your life as a covenant believer in Jesus. The Holy Spirit is forbidding the enemy access to your life in the area of attack and opening the door to what God wants to do instead.

The Message puts it this way: "And that's not all. You will have complete and free access to God's kingdom, keys to open any and every door: no more barriers between heaven and earth, earth and heaven. A yes on earth is yes in heaven. A no on earth is no in heaven."

Jesus once said in Mark 3:27, "No one can enter a strong man's house and plunder his goods, unless he first binds the strong man. And then he will plunder his house." I believe when we pray in tongues, we may be binding a strongman we didn't even know was holding our plunder. I believe when we pray in tongues, we may be positioning ourselves to take back what the enemy stole from us after binding him.

Prayer

Father, in the name of Jesus, thank You for giving me the keys to the Kingdom. As I pray in tongues, would You help me use those keys appropriately? Will You bind the hand of the enemy in my life and loose the Father's perfect will for me?

He Helps You Remember Important Things

When I'm teaching the Word of God or praying on my morning prayer broadcast, rivers of living water flow from my heart and Scripture rolls off my tongue. Sometimes it amazes me how He will pull up a Scripture from the recesses of the Old Testament that I have only read a few times to fit the prayer He's leading me to pray.

How does that happen? Essentially, the Holy Spirit is recalling relevant Scriptures from my spirit according to Psalm 119:11: "Your word I have hidden in my heart." Although I have memorized a lot of Scripture, I haven't memorized all of it. Yet the Holy Spirit reminds me of the pertinent Scriptures so I can pray more precisely.

This is biblical. In John 14:26, Jesus said, "But the Helper, the Holy Spirit, whom the Father will send in My name, He will teach you all things, and bring to your remembrance all things that I said to you." I believe we are more sensitive to the Holy Spirit's nudges when we pray in tongues.

The Passion Translation puts it this way: "But when the Father sends the Spirit of Holiness, the One like me who sets you free, he will teach you all things in my name. And he will inspire you to remember every word that I've told you."

Praying in tongues helps you remember the prophetic words God has spoken over your life and the personal whispers to your heart when you need to remember them most. As we pray in tongues, the Holy Spirit may even remind us of prophecies we long ago set on a shelf.

I walked through a lot of trials in my life. At times, the Holy Spirit would remind me of things that God told me in the past to comfort me. The Holy Spirit can remind you in a still small voice or through another person, but He can also remind you as you pray in tongues. He won't nag you. He'll remind you.

The Holy Spirit will remind you of the goodness of God on a bad day. The Holy Spirit will remind you of the love of God when you feel rejected. The Holy Spirit will remind you of many things you need to know.

But beyond spiritual truths, I have discovered over and over again that the Holy Spirit will remind me of many other things. He will remind me of things I forgot in the natural. For example, now and again I get in a hurry and lay my glasses down somewhere. I can't see without them. That can cause quite a stir when you are late for church!

Over the years, I learned to stop and ask the Holy Spirit where the glasses are (also my keys!). I pray, "Holy Spirit, you know where my glasses are. Please help me find them. You know I need to go to church." Then I pray in tongues. It's uncanny. I usually find them within two minutes. Sometimes they fell behind a shelf, or I put them somewhere I normally don't lay them.

Pray in tongues often and you'll find when you forget you can tap into His memory. He knows everything and never forgets anything.

Prayer

Father, in the name of Jesus, I'm so grateful that You never forget about me and are always willing to remind me of what

I need to know. As I pray in tongues, will You remind me of things I forgot and things I need to focus on to grow in Your Spirit?

Grow More Prophetic

I've been walking in prophetic ministry for decades, yet I continue to pray this prayer: "Lord, make me more prophetic!" And I pray in tongues. I am convinced that the combination of these natural and heavenly language prayers are bearing much and increasing fruit.

I believe that, in part, because when we pray in tongues we are building ourselves up in our most holy faith (see Jude 1:20). When you read Paul's Spirit-inspired words in Romans 12:6, it's not hard to solve this spiritual equation:

> *Having then gifts differing according to the grace that is given to us, let us use them: if prophecy, let us prophesy in proportion to our faith.*

We all have the ability as Spirit-filled believers to prophesy. We have to get trained, activated, and build our faith to prophesy.

You build your faith to prophesy by praying in tongues. Catch this: We all have the ability as Spirit-filled believers to prophesy words of edification, exhortation, and comfort (see 1 Cor. 14:3). You need equipping, impartation, and activation in the prophetic, but you also need to build your faith to prophesy. The greater your faith, the more prolific you will be in prophetic ministry.

The Passion Translation of Romans 12:6 tells us, "So if God has given you the grace-gift of prophecy, activate your gift by using the proportion of faith you have to prophesy."

Of course, you can and should build faith to prophesy by hearing the Word. Paul put it plainly, "So then faith comes by hearing, and hearing by the word of God" (Rom. 10:17). But praying in tongues also builds your faith. It's a one-two punch that will give you more confidence in the accuracy of your prophetic ministry.

I would be remiss if I did not offer this insight: Being prophetic is more than prophesying. Being prophetic is living a life infused with the Holy Spirit's being. Remember, the Holy Spirit is a prophetic Spirit. He prophesies Christ's words to us. He shows us things to come. He warns us when danger is approaching—all prophetic functions.

God wants us to live a prophetic lifestyle under the Holy Spirit's leadership. Being prophetic is knowing what you didn't know, being sensitive to what the Holy Spirit is leading you to do, praying what He wants you to pray. Being prophetic is walking with the ministry of the Holy Spirit activated in your life. Praying in tongues makes you more prophetic.

Put another way, prophesying means speaking forth. You don't prophesy without publishing. You have to speak it or write it or sing it or preach it. But being prophetic doesn't require a spoken word.

Being prophetic could be an inclination to go one way instead of the other. Being prophetic could mean knowing things for the sake of intercession. Being prophetic could mean discerning an atmosphere.

Praying in tongues makes you more prophetic because it is one way we keep ourselves stirred up, alert to the movement of the Spirit, and responsive to His leadership.

Prayer

Father, in the name of Jesus, make me more prophetic. Give me a hunger for Your Word and grace to pray in tongues with a heart to be more sensitive to Your unctions, Your voice, and Your ways.

Speak in Other Languages

When you pray in tongues, you could be praying in a foreign language. I have prayed in tongues at times and heard Middle Eastern languages coming out of my mouth. I've prayed in tongues in Japanese and other languages. How do I know? Because I would look up certain repetitive words and discover they had real meaning. It's amazing.

This is scriptural. We see the first manifestation of tongues that manifest as foreign languages at the birth of the church in Acts 2, better known as the Day of Pentecost. Acts 2:1-12 reads:

> When the Day of Pentecost had fully come, they were all with one accord in one place. And suddenly there came a sound from heaven, as of a rushing mighty wind, and it filled the whole house where they were sitting. Then there appeared to them divided tongues, as of fire, and one sat upon each of them. And they were all filled with the Holy Spirit and began to speak with other tongues, as the Spirit gave them utterance.
>
> And there were dwelling in Jerusalem Jews, devout men, from every nation under heaven. And when this sound occurred, the multitude came together, and were confused, because everyone heard them speak in his own language. Then they were all amazed and marveled, saying to one another, "Look, are not all these who speak Galileans? And how is it that we hear, each in our own language in which we were born? Parthians and Medes and Elamites, those dwelling in Mesopotamia, Judea

and Cappadocia, Pontus and Asia, Phrygia and Pamphylia, Egypt and the parts of Libya adjoining Cyrene, visitors from Rome, both Jews and proselytes, Cretans and Arabs—we hear them speaking in our own tongues the wonderful works of God." So they were all amazed and perplexed, saying to one another, "Whatever could this mean?"

When you pray in tongues, you could be praying in a foreign language. I have been told during *Transform: A 90-Day Spirit Prayer Challenge* that I am praying in African languages, Asian languages, and Middle Eastern languages. I could not interpret it, but others did.

The Passion Translation of Acts 2:11 reads, "Yet we hear them speaking of God's mighty wonders in our own dialects!"

I have a friend, Michelle, who speaks in tongues of French and Chinese. Someone who speaks French told her she was essentially singing praises to God. When her tongues manifest in Chinese, it's clearly a warfare tongue, though we have no idea what she is saying.

As the story is told in a documentary film on the Azusa Street Revival, one of the women at the meeting went to the piano and started to play and sing in the Spirit, though she had never learned to play the piano. The language of music manifested through her hands.

I've had friends who prayed in tongues on altars only to find out they preached a whole message in a foreign language. What's even wilder is they were speaking in English, but it came out in a foreign language. In the end times, God could use the gift of tongues to help people communicate to others who speak different languages. Imagine that!

Prayer

Father, in the name of Jesus, would You help me discern when I am praying in foreign languages when I pray in tongues? Would You help me pray effective prayers through this manifestation of tongues?

Lean on Your Standby in Emergencies

We all need someone who will stand by us through hard times. You'll recall Jesus said He will never leave you or forsake you, even to the end of the age (see Heb. 13:5). Although Jesus ascended to the right hand of the Father in heaven, the spirit of Christ is still in us—and so is the Holy Spirit. Jesus gave us a Standby.

The Amplified Classic translation of John 14:26 says, "But the Comforter (Counselor, Helper, Intercessor, Advocate, Strengthener, Standby), the Holy Spirit, Whom the Father will send in My name [in My place, to represent Me and act on My behalf], He will teach you all things. And He will cause you to recall (will remind you of, bring to your remembrance) everything I have told you."

Have you ever considered this characteristic of the Holy Spirit as Standby? People don't talk about the Holy Spirit as the Standby too often, yet this is a vital aspect of who He is and who He wants us to let Him be in our life.

So what is a standby? *Merriam-Webster*'s dictionary offers some insight. A *standby* is defined as "one to be relied upon especially in emergencies." When you have a 911 situation on your hands, you can count on the Standby to be right there with you, giving you the wisdom, strength, or whatever else you need to navigate the issue as you pray in tongues.

Standby also means "a favorite or reliable choice or resource." The Holy Spirit is my favorite resource. He's certainly reliable. The Holy Spirit is faithful, even when we're not faithful because He cannot deny Himself (see 2 Tim. 2:13).

Paul told the church at Thessalonica, "But the Lord is faithful, who will establish you and guard you from the evil one" (2 Thess. 3:3). When the enemy launches an onslaught against you, the Holy Spirit is standing by to guard you from the evil one as you pray in tongues. He'll never fail you.

The dictionary also defines *standby* as "one that is held in reserve, ready for use." You can activate the Standby in your life through crying out to the Lord, but you can also activate the Standby through praying in tongues.

Stand by means "to be or get ready to act." We don't have to run and hide from trouble. We can stare trouble in the face with confidence that the Holy Spirit will come to our rescue. He is a very present help when we need Him. He is always standing by ready to spring into action when we yield our tongue to His utterance, releasing the perfect cry for assistance in any urgent matter.

Finally, *standby* means "to remain loyal or faith to; defend." The Holy Spirit as Standby is our defender. He is our strong tower in an emergency. He will protect us in the storm. He will shelter us from the enemy. He will defend us to the uttermost. As David said, "The Lord is my rock and my fortress and my deliverer; my God, my strength, in whom I will trust; my shield and the horn of my salvation, my stronghold" (Ps. 18:2).

Prayer

Father, in the name of Jesus, thank You for being my faithful Standby in the emergency. Would You remind me to pray in tongues when my soul is stirring in the face of difficulties? Would You release the perfect prayer of rescue on my behalf?

Walk in Sustained Breakthrough

Want to walk in sustained breakthrough? Praying in tongues consistently will help you manifest a supernatural breakthrough lifestyle.

Let's look at this word *breakthrough* a little more closely. Interestingly enough, the word *breakthrough* is first defined as "an offensive military assault through or beyond an obstacle," according to *Merriam-Webster's* dictionary.

Praying in tongues will help you break through enemy obstacles—even obstacles that you didn't know were there. The Holy Spirit sees the demonic pitfalls and potholes and will help you break through them.

The second definition of *breakthrough* is "a sudden advance especially in knowledge or technique." Praying in tongues consistently will cause you to advance suddenly in the knowledge or techniques you need to succeed.

The third definition of *breakthrough* is "a person's first notable success." Praying in tongues consistently will set you up for your first success—and for success after success after success. God wants you to be successful in everything He leads you to do (see Deut. 30:9). Praying in tongues sets the stage for supernatural success.

I love the Amplified Classic translation of Micah 2:13: "The Breaker [the Messiah] will go up before them. They will break through, pass in through the gate and go out through it, and their King will pass on before them, the Lord at their head."

The Breaker is also your Forerunner. The Breaker goes before you to make a way for you. Praying in tongues makes you more sensitive to the leadership of the Breaker, Jesus.

The Modern English Version of this verse reads, "He who breaks through has gone up before them; they will break through and pass the gate and go out by it. Then their king will pass on before them, the Lord at their head."

When you pray in tongues, you are positioning yourself to follow the Breaker. Paul the apostle put it this way: "Now thanks be to God who always leads us in triumph in Christ, and through us diffuses the fragrance of His knowledge in every place" (2 Cor. 2:14). You might say, God always leads us in triumph in the Breaker.

The New Living Translation says, "Your leader will break out and lead you out of exile, out through the gates of the enemy cities, back to your own land. Your king will lead you; the Lord himself will guide you." The gates of hell will try to prevail against your life—even hold you in bondage—but when you pray in tongues the Breaker will lead you into victory.

Finally, *The Message* relates, "Then I, God, will burst all confinements and lead them out into the open. They'll follow their King. I will be out in front leading them." You wouldn't need a breakthrough if there wasn't some opposition to breakthrough. Whether the opposition is in your mind, in your body, in your family, in your career, or in some other realm, praying in tongues will cause you to bump right into breakthrough.

Prayer

Father, in the name of Jesus, I declare You are my Breaker. As I pray in tongues, would You help me to break through enemy opposition, fleshly opposition, mental opposition and walk in sustained breakthrough?

Release a Sign to Unbelievers

When we think of praying in tongues, we may think of edifying ourselves or making more effective intercession. We may even think about releasing tongues in worship or in times of warfare. But there's another aspect of tongues that is worth noting.

In First Corinthians 14:22, Paul the apostle writes something curious: "So you see that speaking in tongues is a sign, not for believers, but for unbelievers. Prophecy, however, is for the benefit of believers, not unbelievers" (NLT). Many people have trouble with this Scripture. What does it mean?

This doesn't mean you can't prophesy to an unbeliever. It means that speaking in tongues is normal for a Spirit-filled believer. It's not some awe-inspiring manifestation of the Spirit that turns heads, like a miracle might. It's normal.

The Amplified Bible expounds on this: "Therefore, [unknown] tongues are [meant] for a [supernatural] sign, not to believers but to unbelievers [who might be receptive]; while prophecy [foretelling the future, speaking a new message from God to the people] is not for unbelievers but for believers."

This aspect of tongues is not about us, but about those who need to know the Lord and His wondrous works. Unbelievers can't speak in tongues because they are not baptized in the Holy Spirit. God can use us to speak in tongues as a supernatural sign that God is real. *Elliot's*

Commentary for English Readers says, "Tongues were useful to arrest the attention of unbelievers, and, if rightly used, to arouse their convictions."

The Good News Translation puts it this way, "So then, the gift of speaking in strange tongues is proof for unbelievers, not for believers, while the gift of proclaiming God's message is proof for believers, not for unbelievers." And The Voice offers, "So speaking in unknown languages is not a sign to the believing but *a miracle* to the unbelieving; prophecy, though, is not a sign to the unbelieving but for the believing."

This can be difficult to understand, but it's worth understanding. *Barnes' Notes on the Bible* offers some commentary that's worth reading since so many believers have no idea how this verse applies to their lives. Essentially, this relates to tongues that manifest as foreign languages like on the Day of Pentecost. Barnes writes:

> *Are for a sign*—An "indication," an evidence, or a proof that God has imparted this power, and that he attends the preaching of the gospel with his approbation. It is a "sign," or a "miracle," which, like all other miracles, may be designed to convince the unbelieving world that the religion is from God.
>
> *Not to them that believe*—Not to Christians. They are already convinced of the truth of religion, and they would not be benefited by that which was spoken in a language which they could not understand.
>
> *But to them that believe not*—It is a miracle designed to convince them of the truth of the Christian religion. God alone could confer the power of thus speaking; and as it was conferred expressly to aid in the propagation of the gospel, it proved that it was from God.

Prayer

Father, in the name of Jesus, would You use me in this way? Would You manifest foreign languages through my tongues for the sake of getting the attention of lost souls who desperately need to be convinced of the truth of the gospel?

Break Evil Decrees and Curses

Proverbs 26:2 promises, "Like a flitting sparrow, like a flying swallow, so a curse without cause shall not alight." Although Jesus redeemed us from the curse of the law, we can open the door to word curses and evil decrees through sheer disobedience and unrepentant sin.

A curse is a prayer or invocation for harm or injury to come upon one, sometimes in the form of imprecatory prayers—prayers David lifted up to God asking Him to deal with his enemies. An evil decree is wicked, fleshly, and demonic. Like curses, evil decrees aim to cause you harm, misfortune, suffering, sorrow, distress, or calamity.

You can break word curses and evil decrees in the name of Jesus. But sometimes you may not discern evil decrees and curses working against you. But the Holy Spirit does. Whether or not you ever know it, the Holy Spirit can break evil decrees and curses against you as you yield your tongue to His utterance.

A decree is a command or an ordinance. An evil decree is an order that carries the force of demonic law. Goliath cursed David by his gods, but David decreed his victory. God's decree overwhelmed the enemy's decree and Goliath's curse backfired on him.

Curses must be broken. Evil decrees must also be broken and reversed. Praying in tongues can break evil decrees, revoke their impacts, crush curses, and release blessings into your life. The Holy Spirit can pray the perfect prayer through you to shut down these enemy attacks, which often come through the mouths of people who are jealous of us or who harbor anger, resentment, and unforgiveness toward us.

By comparison, God's decrees are just and righteous. God's decrees lead to life and health. God's decrees lead us into His purposes and prosperity. Evil decrees, also called demonic decrees, work the enemy's plans and purposes in our life. God's decrees are congruent with His nature to give us life in abundance, to the full, until it overflows. Evil decrees are congruent with the enemy's nature to steal, kill, and destroy. Evil decrees release evil spirits to enforce the enemy's will in your life. When you pray in tongues, you may be reversing the curses and revoking the decrees.

We see evil decrees throughout the pages of the Bible. Pharaoh decreeing all the male babies be drowned in the water was over fear of losing power. "Pharaoh charged all his people, saying, 'You must cast every son that is born into the river, and you must preserve every daughter's life'" (Exod. 1:22 MEV).

This was a mass slaughter. There were 600,000 men in Egypt, which would lead me to believe there were at least 600,000 women and hundreds of thousands of babies sacrificed to Leviathan in the Nile River during Pharaoh's reign. King Nebuchadnezzar issued a decree that led Shadrach, Meshach, and Abednego into the fiery furnace because people were jealous (see Dan. 3:8-18).

Businesses have failed because of curses and evil decrees. Dreams have been destroyed because of curses and evil decrees. Relationships have failed, finances have collapsed, health has been destroyed, and minds have been tormented because of curses and evil decrees. The good news is, the Holy Spirit sees them even when you don't and can break and reverse them as you pray in tongues.

Prayer

Father, in the name of Jesus, would You teach me to discern curses and evil decrees wreaking havoc on my life? As I pray in tongues, if there be any curses and evil decrees that I am not seeing, would You break and revoke them and set me free from the fruit of these wicked words?

Weather Intense Suffering

Suffering is a part of everyone's life—even believers. Over the years, I've suffered broken legs, broken fingers, broken teeth, broken relationships, and more than once a broken heart. I've been broke financially, felt broke spiritually, and broke emotionally. Praying in tongues helped me weather the storms and suffering—and it will help you make it through too.

Scripture tells us over and over that suffering is part of our walk in this earth. Philippians 1:29 makes it plain: "For to you it has been granted on behalf of Christ, not only to believe in Him, but also to suffer for His sake." And Second Timothy 2:3 tells us, "You therefore must endure hardship as a good soldier of Jesus Christ."

Praying in tongues strengthens us in our inner man so we can endure hardship and suffering. Proverbs 18:14 tells us the spirit of a man can endure his sickness. Much the same, the spirit of a man can endure any kind of suffering through the power of the Holy Ghost. Praying in tongues helps us tap into that endurance.

Sometimes suffering is not physical. Sometimes it's emotional at the hand of those who are jealous or want to see us fail. Second Timothy 3:12 reveals, "Yes, and all who desire to live godly in Christ Jesus will suffer persecution." We can't escape persecution, but we can endure it when we pray in tongues.

Mature Christians eventually get to the point where they can rejoice in suffering. Paul the apostle modeled this maturity: "I now rejoice in my sufferings for you, and fill up in my flesh what is lacking in the afflictions of Christ, for the sake of His body, which is the church" (Col. 1:24). We know Paul prayed in tongues more than anyone (see 1 Cor. 14:18). I believe that helped him rejoice in his many sufferings for the gospel's sake.

When we suffer with a right attitude, we glorify God. First Peter 2:19-21 shows us:

> *For this is commendable, if because of conscience toward God one endures grief, suffering wrongfully. For what credit is it if, when you are beaten for your faults, you take it patiently? But when you do good and suffer, if you take it patiently, this is commendable before God. For to this you were called, because Christ also suffered for us, leaving us an example, that you should follow His steps.*

There's no getting around suffering, but praying in tongues helps us get through it with a mindset that looks toward the next glory. In Romans 8:18 Paul wrote these Spirit-inspired words: "For I consider that the sufferings of this present time are not worthy to be compared with the glory which shall be revealed in us."

God moves us from glory to glory. Although our suffering is far from glorious—it's painful and gut-wrenching—praying in tongues will help us yield to God's perfecting work in the suffering. God will establish us, strengthen us, and settle us in the suffering when we pray in tongues.

Prayer

Father, in the name of Jesus, sometimes the suffering seems too much for me to bear, but You told me in Your Word You will not allow more to come upon me than I can bear. I trust

You. As I pray in tongues, would You help me walk through the suffering with a praise in my mouth?

Cultivate an Eternal Perspective

lthough you live in a house—or an apartment—here on earth, this world is not your home. Hebrews 13:14 tells us plainly, "For this world is not our permanent home; we are looking forward to a home yet to come" (NLT).

Over and over and over, Jesus offered us the promise of eternity with Him. He said, "Most assuredly, I say to you, he who hears My word and believes in Him who sent Me has everlasting life, and shall not come into judgment, but has passed from death into life" (John 5:24).

Jesus also said, "In My Father's house are many mansions; if it were not so, I would have told you. I go to prepare a place for you. And if I go and prepare a place for you, I will come again and receive you to Myself; that where I am, there you may be also" (John 14:2-3).

Paul cultivated an eternal mindset and shared that mindset in his epistles. He told the church at Rome, "For the wages of sin is death, but the gift of God is eternal life in Christ Jesus our Lord" (Rom. 6:23). And to the church at Galatia he wrote, "He who sows to his flesh will of the flesh reap corruption, but he who sows to the Spirit will of the Spirit reap everlasting life" (Gal. 6:8).

Paul went on to tell the church at Philippi, "For our citizenship is in heaven, from which we also eagerly wait for the Savior, the Lord Jesus Christ, who will transform our lowly body that it may be conformed to His glorious body, according to the working by which He is able even to subdue all things to Himself" (Phil. 3:20-21). And to the church at Colossae, he wrote:

> *If then you were raised with Christ, seek those things which are above, where Christ is, sitting at the right hand of God. Set your mind on things above, not on things on the earth. For you died, and your life is hidden with Christ in God. When Christ who is our life appears, then you also will appear with Him in glory* (Colossians 3:1-4).

Praying in tongues helps you cultivate an eternal perspective. I believe one reason Paul had eternity on his mind as a future reality is because he prayed in tongues more than anyone else (see 1 Cor. 14:18). Praying in tongues helps you cut through the clutter, distractions, obstacles, and trials in your current reality so your thinking can ascend to a heavenly perspective.

Cultivating an eternal perspective is vital to our success in the earth. When we suffer, for example, we can quickly lose sight of the reason we're here. We can fall into self-pity and seek comfort from the world rather than from the Spirit of God. We can get frustrated with limitations of life on the earth if we don't keep an eternal perspective that reminds us this is all temporary.

The Passion Translation of Hebrews 13:14 tells us, "For we have no city here on earth to be our permanent home, but we seek the city that is destined to come." Praying in tongues helps you keep eternity in mind— and that changes everything.

Prayer

Father, in the name of Jesus, help me remember that I am a sojourner in the earth, and You have prepared a mansion for me in heaven. As I pray in tongues, help me renew my mind to an eternal perspective that helps me weather the storms of life in this age.

BENEFIT 89

Open Doors
No Man Can Shut

If you've walked with the Lord for any length of time, you know you can't break down doors of opportunity. Even if you force your way through a door, it will cause you nothing but trouble if it's not in the Lord's perfect plan for your life.

Even if it's the right door, trying to walk through the threshold of career, marriage, or other transitions at the wrong time will only frustrate you. When the right door opens, there may be a war to enter the door, but there will be grace to battle through to the other side.

By the same token, there are doors in your life that need to be shut—such as doors to toxic relationships or doors closing on a job path—but you may have a difficult time taking action to shut those doors. Soul ties can make it difficult to leave a person, place, or thing even when you know it's not the best option for your life.

Sometimes, God in His grace and mercy will open doors that you have absolutely no way to open yourself. One way He does this is by speaking to someone who has the authority to open a door of opportunity for you. That person is a divine connection who has the power to essentially roll out the red carpet with great favor. Praying in tongues can lead to those open doors.

I call it the Isaiah 22:22 Key. Isaiah 22:22 reads, "The key of the house of David I will lay on his shoulder; so he shall open, and no one shall shut; and he shall shut, and no one shall open."

Always remember, God opens doors and shuts doors according to His will. Praying in tongues—yielding your voice to His utterance by faith—puts you in agreement with God's plans to open or shut doors. Sometimes doors open and close unexpectedly.

Sometimes it's a divine suddenly at work, even though it hurts to move on as the door closes behind you. But when you pray in tongues you will have peace about going forth. God never closes one door without opening another one.

This key is also called the key of David, which is revealed in Revelation 3:7: "Write the following to the messenger of the congregation in Philadelphia, for these are the solemn words of the Holy One, the true one, who has David's key, who opens doors that none can shut and who closes doors that none can open" (TPT).

Praying in tongues gives you access to doors that you may not find any other way. Praying in tongues prepares your heart to walk through those doors into success, or leave a season of your life with a confidence about what comes next.

Prayer

Father, in the name of Jesus, as I pray in tongues I am coming into agreement with You to open divine doors in Your perfect timing. I am coming into agreement with You to help me shut doors in my life that I don't have the courage to shut—or don't even know need to be shut.

Release Life into Difficult Situations

We know death and life are in the power of the tongue (see Prov. 18:21). Have you ever noticed how most translations of this verse put death before life? I believe that's because our untamed tongues are prone to leaning toward negativity through complaining.

Put another way, our untamed tongues often agree with the vain imaginations the enemy releases at our minds (see 2 Cor. 10:5). In the midst of difficult situations, the enemy puts pressure on our tongue to speak words that agree with his will and thereby give him the right to steal, kill, and destroy (see John 10:10).

When you feel that pressure to speak out the worst-case scenario, pray in tongues. When you feel as if you can't say anything right and it seems impossible to resist the urge to complain, pray in tongues. When you pray in tongues, you are simultaneously releasing life into your situations and shutting down the enemy's attack against your mouth. It's a win-win for you and a lose-lose for the enemy.

The New Living Translation of Proverbs 18:21 reads, "The tongue can bring death or life; those who love to talk will reap the consequences." Our words have consequences. Jesus said, "The words that I speak to you are spirit, and they are life" (John 6:63). Guess what? The prayers the Holy Spirit speaks through you are spirit and life. By contrast, the words of the wicked one are also spirit—spirit and death.

The Passion Translation of Proverbs 18:21 reads, "Your words are so powerful that they will kill or give life, and the talkative person will reap the consequences." Really meditate on that. Really consider the harm or good your words can bring in your life before you open your mouth.

When bad things happen to me, I almost immediately start praying in tongues. It's a habit that has kept me from releasing the power of death over my life and, at the same time, pushed back darkness with words of life from the Holy Spirit's heart.

When I was growing up, my mother used to tell me, "If you can't say anything nice, don't say anything at all." That's wisdom. But I might now say it this way, "If you can't say anything nice, pray in tongues." Sometimes, silence is the answer when a spiritual attack comes. Sometimes you have to bite your tongue to keep from speaking death. But you can one-up the enemy by praying in tongues.

Proverbs 18:4 tells us plainly, "Wise words are like deep waters; wisdom flows from the wise like a bubbling brook " (NLT). The Holy Spirit's words are always life-giving. When we pray in tongues over a difficult situation, we are speaking words of life that overpower the words of death others may be speaking out of ignorance.

And Proverbs 13:3 admonishes us, "He who guards his mouth preserves his life, but he who opens wide his lips shall have destruction." It's easy to cave in to the stress and exhaustion in a trial. You can guard your mouth by yielding your tongue to the Holy Spirit's perfect prayer. You can choose to speak life by submitting your tongue to His utterance.

Prayer

Father, in the name of Jesus, help me resist the temptation to agree with the enemy through my words. When I feel pressure to speak death, would You urge me to pray in tongues so You can speak life-giving words over my life?

Stir Up Your Spiritual Gifts

I will always remember driving over the bridge in Hollywood, Florida, after dropping my daughter off at school. The Lord spoke to me clearly, "I've given you gifts. I expect you to use them." My jaw dropped. I hadn't yet discovered my gifts, but it set me on a journey to explore what He had given me.

When the Lord gives you a gift, He expects you to use it. This is scriptural. First Peter 4:10-11 reads, "As each one has received a gift, minister it to one another, as good stewards of the manifold grace of God. If anyone speaks, let him speak as the oracles of God. If anyone ministers, let him do it as with the ability which God supplies, that in all things God may be glorified through Jesus Christ, to whom belong the glory and the dominion forever and ever. Amen."

Just as you receive the impartation by faith, you must ultimately take action to use the gift by faith. You have to stir yourself up, as Paul told Timothy: "Therefore I remind you to stir up the gift of God which is in you through the laying on of my hands" (2 Tim. 1:6). One way we stir up the gifts God gave us—and the faith to use those gifts—is to pray in tongues.

"Stir up" in the context of this verse comes from the Greek word *anazopureo*, which means "to kindle up, inflame one's mind, strength zeal." In other words, you need to put works with your faith. You need to step out and exercise the gift in a safe setting to build your confidence.

Praying in tongues will bring you confidence to step out in faith and release your gifts for His glory.

The New Living Translation of Second Timothy 1:6 reads, "This is why I remind you to fan into flames the spiritual gift God gave you when I laid my hands on you." With the hectic pace of life, we can easily forget to lend our gifts to the Lord's work in the earth. Praying in tongues helps us stay stirred up.

The Passion Translation puts it this way: "I'm writing to encourage you to fan into a flame and rekindle the fire of the spiritual gift God imparted to you when I laid my hands upon you." Praying in tongues rekindles our fire from within so we can burn and shine for Him.

The Amplified Bible reads, "That is why I remind you to fan into flame the gracious gift of God, [that inner fire—the special endowment] which is in you through the laying on of my hands [with those of the elders at your ordination]." God has given you special endowments. Praying in tongues helps you stay on fire for God as you use your God-given gifts.

Finally, "Do not neglect the spiritual gift you received through the prophecy spoken over you when the elders of the church laid their hands on you" (1 Tim. 4:14 NLT). When you pray in tongues consistently, you won't neglect your gifts.

Prayer

Father, in the name of Jesus, thank You for entrusting me with gifts and talents. It is an honor to serve in Your Kingdom. As I pray in tongues, would You cause me to grow red hot in love so I can share Your gifts with the world around me?

Access Decision-Making Power

Think about this: In any given moment we are either in the will of God or out of the will of God. Whether we are in or out of the will of God is related to the decisions we make. And studies show we make over 35,000 decisions a day.

Many of those decisions are on autopilot—they happen at a subconscious level. For example, we don't have to ask God if we should brush our teeth or take a shower, but there are many decisions every day He wants to be involved in.

Praying in tongues releases decision-making power into our lives. Praying in tongues with a mind toward making right decisions is one means of acknowledging Him in all our ways so that He can direct our paths (see Prov. 3:6).

Some decisions are largely inconsequential, such as what to eat for dinner. But there are major life decisions we have to make as we journey through this earth, such as a career change, answering the call to ministry, who to marry, when to have kids, making major financial purchases, whether or not to move, when to quit (anything), the timing of pursuing new ventures, or even turning down what seems to be a huge opportunity.

In Psalm 32:8, "The Lord says, 'I will guide you along the best pathway for your life. I will advise you and watch over you" (NLT). And the psalmist cried out, "Teach me how to make good decisions, and give me revelation-light, for I believe in your commands" (Ps. 119:66 TPT). Praying in tongues is helps us tap into God's decision-making power so we don't have regrets for missteps.

Proverbs 23:19 reveals, "As you listen to me, my beloved child, you will grow in wisdom and your heart will be drawn into understanding, which will empower you to make right decisions" (TPT). Catch that. God wants to empower us to make right decisions. One way we can tap into that empowerment is by praying in tongues.

Facing the task of decision making can bring anxiety, especially when the decision is monumental and can radically impact your life. Philippians 4:6 tells us, "Be anxious for nothing, but in everything by prayer and supplication, with thanksgiving, let your requests be made known to God." Praying in tongues can ease your anxiety over decision-making so you can keep a cool head.

Let's face it. There are consequences to making bad decisions. While God can work all things together for our good even in the face of our mistakes, we want to do everything we can to make the right choices for our lives—choices that glorify His name.

Proverbs 21:5 makes it plain, "Brilliant ideas pay off and bring you prosperity, but making hasty, impatient decisions will only lead to financial loss" (TPT). Making hasty, impatient decisions in any area of your life typically leads to loss of some sort—whether it's loss of peace, joy, relationships, even jobs. Praying in tongues sets the stage for you to receive decision-making power.

Prayer

Father, in the name of Jesus, I thank You that I am not alone in decision-making but You will help me tap into decision-making power so I can make choices according to Your plans and purposes for my life. As I pray in tongues, please empower me to make the right choices.

Pray Without Ceasing

P ray without ceasing. That's a command—not a suggestion—from First Thessalonians 5:17. Have you ever wondered how that's possible? I have, so I studied it out. I found something intriguing in *Elliott's Commentary for English Readers*: "Though a man cannot be incessantly praying in words, the mind may be held continuously in an attitude of prayer, even in sleep (Song of Solomon 5:2)."

Barnes' Notes on the Bible emphasizes this: "We are to maintain an uninterrupted and constant spirit of prayer. We are to be in such a frame of mind as to be ready to pray publicly if requested; and when alone, to improve any moment of leisure which we may have when we feel ourselves strongly inclined to pray."

Praying in tongues helps us develop an attitude of prayer, so while we're not actually praying all the time—every minute of every day—we are poised to spring into intercession action at the prompting of the Holy Spirit within us.

The New International Version says, "Pray continually." And the New Living Translation, "Never stop praying." And the Amplified Bible relates, "be unceasing and persistent in prayer." The Ethiopic version renders the words, "pray frequently." *Gill's Exposition of the Entire Bible* explains:

> Do not leave off praying, or cease from it through the prevalence of sin, the temptations of Satan, or through discouragement, because an answer is not immediately

had, or through carelessness and negligence, but continue in it, and be often at it.

Praying in tongues helps you stay encouraged in the battle, keeps you from growing weary in well-praying, and makes sure you have all the important bases covered since He's releasing the perfect prayer through you (see Rom. 8:26).

The Good News Translation of First Thessalonians 5:17 tells us, "Pray at all times." *The Message*, "Be cheerful no matter what; pray all the time; thank God no matter what happens. This is the way God wants you who belong to Christ Jesus to live." And *The Passion Translation*, "Make your life a prayer."

I like that. We can make our life a prayer, essentially, when we give ourselves over to praying in tongues. We may be at a loss for words to pray in our native language, but the Holy Spirit is never at a loss for words. He knows the mind of God.

Jesus told us we should always pray and not lose heart (see Luke 18:1). And again, He said, "Watch therefore, and pray always that you may be counted worthy to escape all these things that will come to pass, and to stand before the Son of Man" (Luke 21:36). Finally, Paul echoes in Romans 12:12, "Rejoicing in hope, patient in tribulation, continuing steadfastly in prayer."

Apart from the Holy Spirit's help, we can't pray without ceasing. We can't continue steadfastly in prayer. Apart from the Holy Spirit's help, we can't make our life a prayer. We will grow weary. But when we pray in tongues, He strengthens us to overcome our weak flesh and our tired soul to pray always.

Prayer

Father, in the name of Jesus, I love when You help me pray. I love when You pray through me. As I pray in tongues, would You help me tap into the spirit of prayer? Would You make me more sensitive to Your leading into intercession? I want to pray always.

Get the Help You Need

We all need God's help—probably more than we realize. Apart from Him, we can do nothing (see John 15:5). Thank God, we were not left as orphans when Jesus ascended to the right hand of the Father. We have the Holy Spirit, the ultimate helper.

Jesus made it crystal clear: "But the Helper, the Holy Spirit, whom the Father will send in My name, He will teach you all things, and bring to your remembrance all things that I said to you" (John 14:26).

Helper in this verse comes from the Greek word *parakletos*. One of the definitions of *parakletos* is "summoned, called to one's side, esp., called to one's aid," according to *The KJV New Testament Greek Lexicon*. It also means, "in the widest sense, a helper, succorer, aider, assistant."

When we pray in tongues, we may be summoning the Holy Spirit's help with issues we don't even know we need help with. Praying in tongues calls on the Holy Spirit, the Helper, within us to come to our aid and assist us in times of need.

David understood this characteristic of God. He wrote, "Behold, God is my helper; the Lord is with those who uphold my life" (Ps. 54:4). And again, "But I am poor and needy; yet the Lord thinks upon me. You are my help and my deliverer; do not delay, O my God" (Ps. 40:17).

Praying in tongues helps us catch the revelation of the Holy Spirit as helper and gives us confidence that He will show up in times of trouble with the aid and assistance we need. Praying in tongues helps us avoid the trap of fear when overwhelming circumstances rise up in our path.

I love Isaiah 41:10, which tells us: "Fear not, for I am with you; be not dismayed, for I am your God. I will strengthen you, yes, I will help you, I will uphold you with My righteous right hand." That's a promise. We can cry out to God for help in any moment. We can also pray in tongues and activate the Helper's assistance.

Psalm 46:1 tells us, "God is our refuge and strength, a very present help in trouble." Psalm 121:1-2 reminds, "I will lift up my eyes to the hills—from whence comes my help? My help comes from the Lord, who made heaven and earth." God is everywhere all the time. Praying in tongues makes us more aware of His presence—and His help.

Do you need relief from something that seems unbearable? Rescue from a difficult situation? Emotional support in the midst of a trial? The Holy Spirit is your helper. Praying in tongues delivers the help when we need it.

It's another way we can walk in Hebrews 4:16, "Let us therefore come boldly to the throne of grace, that we may obtain mercy and find grace to help in time of need." The Holy Spirit is the Spirit of Grace (see Zech. 12:10). His grace will help you. Praying in tongues activates that grace.

Prayer

Father, in the name of Jesus, I need all the help I can get, though I don't always recognize how helpless I am without You. As I pray in tongues, would You provide me the help, aid, and assistance I need to succeed in what You've called me to do, in my relationships, and in other realms of life?

Do the Greater Works

Jesus pointed to specific signs that would follow believers: "In My name they will cast out demons; they will speak with new tongues; they will take up serpents; and if they drink anything deadly, it will by no means hurt them; they will lay hands on the sick, and they will recover" (Mark 16:17-18).

If that's all He promised, most of us would be satisfied with these supernatural expressions. But that's not all Jesus said. In John 14:12 He made an even more astounding statement: "Most assuredly, I say to you, he who believes in Me, the works that I do he will do also; and greater works than these he will do, because I go to My Father."

Praying in tongues prepares you for the greater works. That's because praying in tongues builds you up in your most holy faith (see Jude 20). Praying in tongues rids your heart of doubt, unbelief, and fear of stepping into the greater works.

The Passion Translation of John 14:12 puts it this way, "I tell you this timeless truth: The person who follows me in faith, believing in me, will do the same mighty miracles that I do—even greater miracles than these because I go to be with my Father!"

If we didn't have doubt or unbelief that we could walk in the greater miracles, we would be operating at a higher plane. Praying in tongues helps us ascend beyond our mental assent that miracles are for today and start stepping into these promises for Christ's glory.

The Amplified Bible relates, "I assure you and most solemnly say to you, anyone who believes in Me [as Savior] will also do the things that I do; and he will do even greater things than these [in extent and outreach], because I am going to the Father."

Have you ever wondered what these greater works are? There is plenty of debate among theologians about what this means. Some argue the disciples would do more impressive, more dramatic miracles.

Specifically, they point to Pentecost, where believers were speaking in foreign languages (see Acts 2). They point to Acts 5:15: "They brought the sick out into the streets and laid them on beds and couches, that at least the shadow of Peter passing by might fall on some of them." They also point to Acts 19:12: "Even handkerchiefs or aprons were brought from his body to the sick, and the diseases left them and the evil spirits went out of them."

Others argue it's the collective preaching of the gospel that brings forth salvation and the spread of Christianity, with thousands saved in Peter's first message after Pentecost. Still others point to greater quantity rather than quality of works.

Praying in tongues sets the stage for us to pray the perfect prayer that releases us into the greater works. Praying in tongues stirs us up and makes us more sensitive to His prompting to step out in faith in Jesus' name.

Prayer

Father, in the name of Jesus, I want to make a maximum impact for Jesus in this earth. I want to do the greater works to demonstrate that Jesus is alive. As I pray in tongues, will You root out any fear, doubt, or unbelief that is holding me back from stepping out in faith at Your leading to work the works of the Christ?

Discern the Voice of Devils

There's never been a single moment in time when the Holy Spirit doesn't know what the enemy is up to in your life. He's never caught off guard by phonies pretending to be your friend. He always discerns the motives of people's hearts and the work of demons to influence people against you.

We don't always discern the motives of the voices in the spirit speaking to us. There are many voices in the realm of the spirit, and they are not all speaking on behalf of God. Demons can mimic God's still small voice to deceive you and trap you—but, thankfully, the Holy Spirit sees right through it.

Don't you wish you could say the same? The reality is, none of us perfectly discern devils despite the fact that John the Beloved tells us put spirits to the test: "Beloved, do not believe every spirit, but test the spirits, whether they are of God; because many false prophets have gone out into the world" (1 John 4:1).

Discerning the spirits speaking through a prophet—or any person you are dealing with—is vital. From used car salesmen trying to get one over on you to discerning flattery and manipulation from a coworker and beyond, we are charged with discerning spirits.

The Passion Translation of First John 4:1 tells us, "Delightfully loved friends, don't trust every spirit, but carefully examine what they say to determine if they are of God, because many false prophets have mingled into the world."

Notice how much of discerning demons occurs through what is said. As Derek Prince taught, "Demons are persons without bodies, and persons have a voice." Demons have voices and their words release vain imaginations against your mind (see 2 Cor. 10:5).

When we don't discern those false voices—which often shame us, guilt us, condemn us, tempt us, or otherwise deceive us under the direction of the father of lies—we can end up in the enemy's trap. When we don't discern the spirit behind the words people speak, we can lose time, money, relationships, and more.

Think of the young prophet in First Kings 13. He was on assignment for the Lord to deliver a rebuke to King Jeroboam. He successfully completed his mission and was on his way home when an elder prophet caught up with him and tempted him to defy the Lord's command to go back home a different way. First Kings 13:18-19 tells the story:

> But the old prophet answered, "I am a prophet, too, just as you are. And an angel gave me this command from the Lord: 'Bring him home with you so he can have something to eat and drink.'" But the old man was lying to him. So they went back together, and the man of God ate and drank at the prophet's home (NLT).

The old prophet was lying to the younger prophet, but the younger prophet—as prophetic as he was—didn't test the spirits. His fate: He was eaten by a lion because of his disobedience in the mission. Don't believe everything anyone says, prophet or not. Pray in tongues and discern the spirit behind the words.

Prayer

Father, in the name of Jesus, I don't want to operate in suspicion but I can't afford to be deceived by people with ill intentions or vain imaginations the enemy releases against my mind to bind me. As I pray in tongues, would You help me test the spirits behind the words I am hearing?

Dig a Well Within

I've traveled all over the world preaching the gospel, building houses of prayer, and raising up prophetic people. When I'm in go-mode, I don't always have the opportunity to spend several hours in the morning sitting in the presence of God, reading His Word, and praying.

While I do my devotions and pray during travel, I'm also pouring out much more than I am taking in. In other words, I am teaching, preaching, praying, and prophesying over people for much longer than I am waiting on the Lord in my hotel room each day.

But as I explained in *The Prophet's Devotional*, I've learned the secret to sustaining a deep, accurate prophetic ministry despite the very real challenges of travel: I dig a well while I'm home so I can draw from it when my pace is more hectic. Then I prime the pump on the well while I'm on the road.

What do I mean by digging a well and what is your well? You may never have seen it this way, but you have a well within you. A well in the natural is a hole that issues water from the earth. Spiritually speaking, your well is your spirit man. The more you pray in tongues, the more you dig that well within—the capacity to receive prophetic intelligence from the Holy Spirit for your life and enough to pour out to others.

Put another way, praying in tongues expands your spiritual capacity. It adds depth to your well. So does meditating on the Word of God, praise and worship, or just sitting in His presence, where you can tap into fullness of joy, peace, courage, or whatever else you need on your journey.

But let's focus on praying in tongues, because it's easy enough to do that anywhere you are. It's one way you can literally pray without ceasing (see 1 Thess. 5:16-18). Jesus said:

> *He who believes in Me [who cleaves to and trusts in and relies on Me] as the Scripture has said, From his innermost being shall flow [continuously] springs and rivers of living water. But He was speaking here of the Spirit, Whom those who believed (trusted, had faith) in Him were afterward to receive. For the [Holy] Spirit had not yet been given, because Jesus was not yet glorified (raised to honor)* (John 7:38-39 AMPC).

The enemy wants to stop up your well with business, stress, fatigue, or even fleshly desires. He'll do anything he can to dry up your well. We see this concept in the life of Isaac. He kept trying to re-dig the wells of his father Abraham, but the locals kept tempting him into strife. Isaac persevered despite enemy opposition and succeeded in cultivating a well that would leave him and his camp well watered. Make digging a well your priority in the quiet times so you can draw from its depths in the busy times.

Prayer

Father, in the name of Jesus, remind me to take advantage of the time I have in Your presence. Remind me to pray in tongues, knowing that I am expanding my capacity to receive from You so I can continue to minister to Your people when the pace seems too frenzied to dig.

Fulfill Your Prophetic Destiny

You have a prophetic destiny, and God is cheering you on as you set out to fulfill it. We all want to hear Jesus say "Well done, good and faithful servant" at the end of the age. Praying in tongues helps you walk in and ultimately fulfill your prophetic destiny.

What do I mean by prophetic destiny? The destiny God had in mind for you since before the creation of the earth. Ephesians 1:11 tells us, "In Him also we have obtained an inheritance, being predestined according to the purpose of Him who works all things according to the counsel of His will."

Part of the Holy Spirit's role in your life is to see that you walk in your prophetic destiny. In order to walk in—and walk out—your prophetic destiny, you have to allow the Holy Spirit to shift your mindsets and purify your heart to agree with His agendas. As I write in my book *Walking in Your Prophetic Destiny*, often that sounds like "Not my will, but yours be done, Lord."

Ephesians 2:10 tells us, "We have become his poetry, a re-created people that will fulfill the destiny he has given each of us, for we are joined to Jesus, the Anointed One. Even before we were born, God planned in advance our destiny and the good works we would do to fulfill it!" (TPT).

When we pray in tongues, we are yielding to the Holy Spirit's work in our hearts to sanctify us, convict us of sin, remind us what Jesus taught, and more. When we pray in tongues, we are submitting to His leadership and to Christ's plans for our life.

Proverbs 2:9 reveals, "Then you will discover all that is just, proper, and fair, and be empowered to make the right decisions as you walk into your destiny" (TPT). The Holy Spirit is the one who empowers us to make right decisions as we walk in our prophetic destiny.

Proverbs 20:24 reinforces this: "It is the Lord who directs your life, for each step you take is ordained by God to bring you closer to your destiny. So much of your life, then, remains a mystery!" (TPT). I believe the more we pray in tongues, the more clarity we have into God's direction for our lives. We essentially leave our destiny and its timing in God's hands (see Ps. 16:5 TPT).

Of course, the enemy comes to distract us from our prophetic destiny. He does this with distractions, delays, and all manner of spiritual warfare. The Holy Spirit sees him coming and warns us. He helps us stay focused on that narrow path that leads to life (see Matt. 7:14).

Sometimes we mistakenly think we know what's best for our lives and charge ahead after some desire in our heart that God never planted. Proverbs 19:21 explains, "A person may have many ideas concerning God's plan for his life, but only the designs of his purpose will succeed in the end" (TPT). The more we pray in tongues, the more likely we are to accurately walk with Him toward our prophetic destiny.

Prayer

Father, in the name of Jesus, I want to accomplish all the work You sent me to the earth realm to complete. As I pray in tongues, would You give me the revelation, the leading, the guiding, the conviction, and the confidence I need to walk in my prophetic destiny?

Release the Perfect Decree

We find a powerful truth in Job 22:28, "Thou shalt also decree a thing, and it shall be established unto thee: and the light shall shine upon thy ways" (KJV). When you pray in tongues, you can release the perfect decree.

A decree is "an order usually having the force of law," according to *Merriam-Webster*'s dictionary. But it seems decrees don't always carry the weight in the natural realm they should. Make no mistake, though, decrees do carry weight in the spirit realm.

When you pray in tongues, you may be releasing the perfect decree. It's the same concept of praying the perfect prayer in Romans 8:26-27:

> *In the same way the Spirit [comes to us and] helps us in our weakness. We do not know what prayer to offer or how to offer it as we should, but the Spirit Himself [knows our need and at the right time] intercedes on our behalf with sighs and groanings too deep for words. And He who searches the hearts knows what the mind of the Spirit is, because the Spirit intercedes [before God] on behalf of God's people in accordance with God's will* (AMP).

In order to see Job 22:28 come to pass—in order to see the decree you release establish God's will in a situation—it has to be a Spirit-inspired decree. In other words, we can't just choose to decree what we want when we want and expect God to back it up. So when we feel led to decree but we don't know what to decree, we can pray in tongues.

I do that because I know the Holy Spirit can release the perfect decree from our mouth when we yield our tongue to His utterance. Essentially, it's a prophetic decree that you may never understand, but when God's will is established in a situation and you're not sure exactly how, it's possible your tongues released prayers and decrees that settled the matter.

As I explain my book *Decrees That Make the Devil Flee, gazar* is the Hebrew word for *decree* in Job 22:28. *Gazar* means "to cut, divide, cut down, cut off, cut in two, snatch." When we decree, we are cutting off the enemy's plan and establishing God's will. Decrees release judgment against the enemy. Decrees shift circumstances. Decrees may even release angels to war on your behalf.

Different translations shed interesting light on this verse. For example, the New International Version tells us, "What you decide on will be done, and light will shine on your ways." The Contemporary English Version puts it this way: "He will do whatever you ask, and life will be bright." And *The Message* puts it this way: "You'll pray to him and he'll listen; he'll help you do what you've promised. You'll decide what you want and it will happen; your life will be bathed in light."

We can decree like God, as long as we're decreeing His will. We can decree the decrees of God, the Word of God, and what the Holy Spirit leads us to decree. When we pray in tongues with a heart to make the perfect decree—or when we pray in tongues when inspired—we could be shifting circumstances we didn't even know existed.

Prayer

Father, in the name of Jesus, I don't always know how to decree as I ought, but You know what needs to be established in my life. Would You decree the perfect prayer through me as I pray in tongues?

BENEFIT 100

Activate the Ministry
of Angels

Angels are ministering spirits and are ready and waiting to minister to the heirs of salvation (see Heb. 1:14). The word *angel* is mentioned in the Bible over 280 times. That's an average of over four times for each of the 66 books in the Bible. If the Lord were to pull back the spirit realm, you would see angels all around.

As heirs of salvation, we must understand the many functions of angels and cooperate with the Lord and His angels to see His good, perfect, and acceptable will come to pass in our lives.

Know this: There are different times and reasons and seasons to activate specific angels on assignment in your life. I believe the Holy Spirit gives us an unction or a leading to activate those angels by praying His Word and declaring His will. When we're sensitive to the Holy Spirit's voice, we will discern the unction to release angels to function.

Psalm 103:20 says, "Praise the Lord, you angels, you mighty ones who carry out his plans, listening for each of his commands" (NLT). The angels are listening for God's commands. When we speak the Word, angels' ears perk up. Likewise, when we pray in tongues, we may be activating the ministry of angels in our lives because the Holy Spirit is releasing the perfect prayer through us.

The Passion Translation of Psalm 103:20 reads, "So bless the Lord, all his messengers of power, for you are his mighty heroes who listen intently to the voice of his word to do it."

It's important to note that we don't command angels. Jesus is the Captain of the Hosts and they respond to His Word. This is one of the ways God watches over His word to perform it (see Jer. 1:12). The angels execute God's commands. When we pray in tongues, we may be releasing the command of Christ to deploy angelic hosts.

The Message version of Psalm 103:20-22 will open your eyes wider:

> *God has set his throne in heaven; he rules over us all. He's the King! So bless God, you angels, ready and able to fly at his bidding, quick to hear and do what he says. Bless God, all you armies of angels, alert to respond to whatever he wills. Bless God, all creatures, wherever you are—everything and everyone made by God. And you, O my soul, bless God!*

I believe when we pray in tongues we can, as the Holy Spirit wills, deploy angel armies on our behalf or on behalf of others in the realm of intercession. We may never know what we're doing, but that's OK. We're yielding our tongue to His utterance and He does what's necessary.

When you are in warfare, pray in tongues and bless the Lord. Know that when you give voice to His prayer through you, if you need angels to come to the rescue they will. While it's not up to you to order the angels, the Holy Spirit can use your mouth to release the prayer in God's will that causes them to act on the Word.

Prayer

Father, in the name of Jesus, when I find myself in spiritual warfare, would You remind me to pray in tongues. And as I pray in tongues, I will trust You to do what You will, whether it's giving me revelation, strengthening me for battle, or sending angels to fight for and with me.

Shut Down the Accuser of the Brethren

Our adversary the devil, who roams about like a roaring lion seeking someone to devour, is also our accuser. Another name for satan is the "accuser of the brethren." Revelation 12:10 speaks of his sinister operation: "the accuser of our brethren, who accused them before our God day and night."

Catch that. Day and night accusations. Satan launches a never-ending stream of accusations, which are legal charges of wrong doing. In other words, the enemy is quick to report our sins, offenses, trespasses, violations, and misbehavior to our heavenly Father.

Sounds grim, huh? Thanks to be God, the Holy Spirit is our Advocate. Jesus said, "But when the Father sends the Advocate as my representative—that is, the Holy Spirit—he will teach you everything and will remind you of everything I have told you" (John 14:26 NLT). While Jesus is advocating for you in heaven, the Holy Spirit can advocate for you on earth.

Praying in tongues activates the Holy Spirit as Advocate. He can convict people who are tapping into the mind of the accuser of the brethren to accuse you, malign you, slander you, and otherwise harm you with persecuting words. As you pray in tongues, the Holy Spirit can come to your defense with people.

You need to see the power of the word *advocate*. According to *Merriam-Webster's* dictionary, an advocate is "one who pleads the cause of another; one who defends or maintains a cause or proposal, or one who supports or promotes the interests of a cause or group."

While Jesus is pleading your case based on His shed blood at Calvary's cross as the original Advocate (see 1 John 2:1), the Holy Spirit is advocating from within you. The Holy Spirit is releasing the perfect prayer for you based on Christ's sacrifice for you.

You might say, "Well, I live a very clean life. Satan has nothing of which to accuse me." But Romans 3:23 tells us we have all sinned and fallen short of the glory of God. We can sin in thought, word, or deed. There are sins of commission—things you do—and sins of omission—things you ought to do but don't do. Much of our sin has nothing to do with what we do but what we think and speak.

When we don't think on "whatever things are true, whatever things are noble, whatever things are just, whatever things are pure, whatever things are lovely, whatever things are of good report, if there is any virtue and if there is anything praiseworthy" according to Philippians 4:8, we're sinning.

Then there's our mouth. Jesus said, "But I tell you, on the day of judgment men will have to give account for every idle (inoperative, nonworking) word they speak. For by your words you will be justified and acquitted, and by your words you will be condemned and sentenced" (Matt. 12:36-37 AMPC).

When you pray in tongues, your words will never be idle, inoperative, and nonworking. When you pray in tongues, you will be justified and acquitted from the enemy's accusations against you in thought, word, and deed.

Prayer

Father, in the name of Jesus, thank You that You are my Advocate and not my accuser. You are the One who convicts and does not condemn. As I pray in tongues, would You advocate for me against the accuser of the brethren?

ABOUT
JENNIFER LECLAIRE

Jennifer LeClaire is senior leader of Awakening House of Prayer in Fort Lauderdale, Florida, founder of the Ignite Network, and founder of the Awakening Prayer Hubs prayer movement. Jennifer formerly served as the first-ever female editor of *Charisma* magazine and is a prolific author of over 50 books. You can find Jennifer online or shoot her an email at info@jenniferleclaire.org.